PSYCHOLOGY OF

FUNERAL SERVICE

By
EDWARD A. MARTIN, B.A.
Mortician

SIXTH EDITION

•

First Edition . . . . 2,000 Copies

Second Edition . . . . 3,000 Copies

Third Edition . . . . 5,000 Copies

Fourth Edition . . . . 5,000 Copies

Fifth Edition . . . . 5,000 Copies

Sixth Edition . . . . 3,000 Copies

Printed by
COLORADO PRINTING COMPANY
Grand Junction, Colorado

CONTENTS

CONTENTS, Continued

CONTENTS, Continued

Chapter   Page

CONTENTS, Continued

CONTENTS, Continued

CONTENTS, Continued

PROLOGUE

EDUCATION

A great deal has been said for many years about education; raising of standards, better and more adequate and thorough training of our students. No doubt everything that was said was spoken with great intentions. Everybody agreed on the general phraseology.

What is meant by education? To educate is to train in a skill, to teach facts. Probably everyone will agree up to this point, also. But is not education more than this?

First of all, to be educated is to be mature. That is one of the reasons for spending so many years in school studying books and listening to lectures, not for the facts learned as much as to allow the individual time to "grow up."

Once the individual has become more nearly mature, then the purpose of education is to enable him to live in understanding with all men. Education, then is an attitude which is constantly maintained by an individual toward his surroundings, toward all other persons.

This attitude of understanding toward all creatures is at once an attitude of tolerance and patience, tolerance of the sincere beliefs held by others, patience with those who have not reached maturity in their learning attitudes.

Education is more than teaching an individual to perform some specific task; it prepares him to live a well-rounded life, capable of mingling with all mankind, regardless of race, creed, training or culture. An education does more than teach a man some specific branch of knowledge; it also teaches him to live at peace with his neighbors. In a short time, a few weeks or months, an average man can learn the known facts of one line of endeavor sufficiently to earn a livelihood; but to mature, an individual needs a long period of time in which to learn to understand the world in which he lives, and many there are who never reach this understanding.

Training must of necessity include specialized instruction in the performance of certain specified tasks and skills, but its background must be a broad and cultural foundation. In government this means that there may be one truth for the whole nation, with no one political party having a monopoly of it. In religion it means that no one church or group has sole access to truth. In academic matters it means that we all owe allegiance to a common truth, with no one department of learning having sole grasp of it.

The primary objective of education should not be merely to train young men to be lawyers, doctors, engineers, morticians, business men, teachers, or scholars. Rather it should give them, through guidance and discipline, access to the riches and skill in the use of human experience for the ennobling of their lives. It is through such training that a free society may best learn how to keep itself free, how by self-control to avoid state control and all the bigotry that goes with it.

Should civilization fail, and it may, it will not be for lack of men technically competent in routine labors;

it will fail for lack of men capable of looking above and beyond that circumscribed horizon of prejudice and self-interest.

It has been wisely said that education makes a people easy to lead but difficult to drive, easy to govern but impossible to enslave. Education teaches individuals to think, to think independently and also with others, for the best interests of all.

It is apparent that technological and scientific development has far outstripped the knowledge of social relationships. Men have been intent on unraveling the mysteries of nature, but have yet to achieve an adequate formula for living together in a common brotherhood. Some of the time spent in acquiring sufficient knowledge to enable a person to learn the means of earning a livelihood certainly should be devoted to acquiring a cultural education to assist in establishing a more universal social consciousness. It is the responsibility of education to so mould the thoughts of students that the common rights and mutual interests of all individuals will be recognized as essential to survival.

To become educated is not to rush through a technical training institution in the shortest possible time, merely to learn a few facts of a specialized skill or vocation. To become educated is to allow sufficient time for the individual to become mature, not only in his chronological age, but in his ability to understand life, his fellow man and the world about him.

MORTUARY EDUCATION

"What kind of a person do we want when we turn out a finished product to serve the public as a mortician?"

The answer to this question is the answer to the question as to how much and what kind of education should we provide for mortuary students. "As the twig is bent so the tree grows" is an adage that applies to the training we give to future morticians.

True education takes cognizance of all of the needs of man so as to develop a rightly integrated personality. When we visualize the funeral director of the future we must realize that a broad, liberal educational background is imperative. The funeral director must be a diversified individual. As such, a broad, academic foundation will enhance his professional and social stature. More emphasis must be placed on training that will assist in understanding himself, his client and the social and economic environment. Our primary goal must be to turn out graduates who will become intelligently progressive leaders within the profession, as well as in their respective communities.

In a great human service field such as funeral service, the ability of a man to work with people, to understand them and to serve them becomes a prime requisite. Higher education is becoming a greater factor. This has been the trend for a long period of time. Other things being equal, the man with higher education is given preference in all lines of endeavor. While college education was not usual among those who reached the top in business and industry in the earlier periods of our nation's growth, the situation today is vastly different. A survey of our nation's leaders in industry today shows them to be men of higher education.

With the national educational average so rapidly rising, we must keep our own standards in advance of those we serve. Otherwise, how can we adequately serve them? How can we maintain their respect if we do not possess qualifications above average?

Education is the main determining factor in the future welfare of our profession, the only road to higher standards. It is the key that opens the door to better service, to greater opportunity. This, in turn, generates higher public esteem of our profession, greater public satisfaction in our service. Living at a time when mass education is constantly and continually becoming higher, our preparation for living as successful citizens necessitates our maintaining standards above the average. Nothing less can be accepted.

PREFACE

When people in grief must be served, the principles of such service must be based on sound psychological knowledge. The intimate relationships that exist between the funeral director and his grief-stricken clients demand careful treatment. While the study of psychology will not guarantee success in these relationships, any more than a study of economics will guarantee financial success, it will greatly help. The personality of the funeral director is, of course, the greatest factor, but a knowledge of psychology will be of the utmost value in assisting him toward a more understanding attitude in his contacts with those who call upon him for service.

Actually, the science of psychology is simple in application. It is nothing more than an understanding of how and why individuals react to certain conditions or stimuli. It is an analysis of human behavior. To use psychology advantageously in dealing with people calls for little more than applied common sense and an understanding of human behavior.

Applying common sense to funeral service means, first, an understanding by the mortician of the emotions of bereaved families and how they react to the stimulus of grief and, second, giving a service that will satisfy and relieve the emotional and unusual situation in which they are placed. It will enable him to be a better mortician.

Whether he realizes it or not every successful mortician is successful in the application of psychological principles. The foundation of the funeral service profession is embalming and the basis of financial profit is merchandising. But the entire public relations program upon which every funeral establishment depends for its continued existence rests upon the soundness of the psychological practices of the management and personnel of that mortuary. Whether one recognizes his successful principles as psychological or not, whether he knows anything about psychology as it is taught in books or not, does not matter. Some men are good psychologists and do not know it. The fact does remain, however, that a study of psychology as such and its application in contact with other people will help any person in his public relationships.

The more we know about people the better we can serve them. The more we understand the reactions of people to their experiences, the better we know the functioning of their minds and their feelings. With this knowledge we can assist them through the period of bereavement. We know that people are generally emotionally upset when they call us for our service. It is our purpose as morticians to give to those we serve a memory picture of their tragic experience that will leave them with comforting thoughts in the years to come. If we do this our services to them will have been worth more than words or money can express; if we fail in this our services were meaningless. We serve people at a time when they need comfort, counsel and direction.

The mortician must endeavor to meet the challenge of keeping the sentimental expressions of people directed in the paths that will be productive of the greatest good for them in their attempt to meet and solve the problems arising as a result of a loss by death in their circle. These finer sensibilities must be preserved. There is no better place to preserve them than in tributes of respect to the memory of their dead.

CHAPTER I

INTRODUCTION

The Study of Psychology

Psychology is the latest science to be developed. Man has studied last that which is within him. This was natural, because the things he could see and feel aroused his curiosity first; he did not wonder **why** he acted as he did because he was so interested in studying his surroundings.

Tangible substance is much easier to study than the intangible. It is natural that early man would explore the world about him, even the distant worlds that he could see, rather than attempt to explore the recesses of his own mind. The reaction of one chemical substance with another, the physics of falling bodies, of weights and measures, the movements of the stars, the attempt to master mathematical formulas, all these held more interest, more romance for mankind than even the thought that he pry into the one thing responsible for his actions, his mind. He worked first with things he could see and with objects that he could touch. Those results were plain and beyond dispute when accomplished. His own reactions were taken for granted.

Except for superficial observation, early man gave no thought to the reason for the actions of himself or his fellow man. He knew that certain acts by him would anger his neighbor and would cause him to fight. He knew that certain happenings caused him to flee, to seek safety, but he did not know why he trembled after the danger was past. He experienced feelings of grief at the loss of a member of his family or a friend, but he did not understand, nor did he attempt to understand, the feeling of frustration arising from his inability to remedy the situation.

Study of Man

Primitive man was probably more easily excited and upset than is modern man for the same reason that a small child is more deeply affected by pains and pleasures than is a present-day adult. Early man, like the child of today, lived only in the present, could not reason in the future. If adversity struck him, he could see nothing else, could not realize that present circumstances would soon pass. He was more deeply affected by his emotions because the present was all-important to him. When he became hungry his only reaction was to go out and hunt food, to eat until his hunger was satisfied. He was slow learning to compare past happenings to similar circumstances of the present. He lived in the present.

Of all living organisms, man is the most complex and is the most difficult to understand. His actions are the least predictable because he is the most highly developed, because he thinks for himself. He measures present situations by past experiences. His reactions are more than mere physical reactions; they are the basic reactions of his physical organism plus a personal response that comes from his intelligence. Man acts, discriminates, senses, understands, reasons and imagines. While lower forms of life have the potentialities of these powers, all more or less developed, man uses them to a higher degree. Man has the ability to reason in the abstract, to think of things unseen. This explains the development of religion, of ethics. Man's imagination is responsible for the expanding of scientific progress.

Except for parental protection of the young, what living organism other than man protects the weak, nurses the sick, attempts to heal the wounded? These are signs of man's developed civilization. He has learned that such things are good and proper. He is able to conceive the principle of a "Golden Rule," to place himself in his imagination in the position of one less fortunate, to show pity for the unprotected.

Psychology endeavors to collect reliable information about the nature, sources and development of the behavior of man. Civilized man is interested in studying himself. Psychology is the study of self, of one's own self and other selves, of the reaction of these selves to one another and to their environment. Since the world, or the environment, is constantly changing, it is necessary that living organisms be able to alter behavior to meet new circumstances in order to survive. This explains why some species of life have become extinct: they were not able to change with their ever-changing environment. This has been true down through the ages, from the dinosaur down to some recent extinct specimens, the dodo bird, and many others familiar to scientists. Many are the primitive tribes that have become extinct because of their inability to cope with conditions imposed upon them by the white man when he invaded their domain. In order to survive, then, man must continue to be able to cope with his environment, to change, to adapt himself to changing conditions.

Psychology Defined

Psychology is the science that studies the activities of living organisms in relation to their environment. Since the word 'psychology' comes from two Greek words meaning 'the science of the mind,' then a study of psychology properly seeks the mental reaction to environment. There are many physiological conditions that must also be studied, for the brain, being an organ of the body, works in close harmony with all of the other organs, with the total body.

The brain can be compared to the person driving a motor car. The car can travel down the highway without anyone at the wheel to guide it, the same as the body of an individual can function if that individual loses his mind, goes insane; but without guidance the motor car would soon wreck and become valueless, just so the body is of no value without the intelligent guidance of the normal brain, the mind.

It is necessary to do more than just observe actions and reactions in the study of psychology. Common, superficial observation is not a sufficient guide to a reliable knowledge of human affairs. Such observation is colored by preconceptions and prejudices. After observations are made and data are compiled it is necessary to study the reason for certain reactions, to know something of the background and heredity of the individual, and to understand the reaction of the total organism.

Mental reaction to every experience affects the organs of the body, the glands and their secretions, the heartbeat, the circulation of the blood, the functional working of every organ of the body. Every organ of the body, being dependent upon every other organ is affected by any change, and all are controlled by the brain and nervous system.

No simple response ends with the termination of the observable physical action. Every stimulus, every experience, makes a definite impression on the individual's memory. The influence of every experience alters the remainder of that individual's life. To understand total reactions of individuals is the purpose of psychology.

The human organism is a totality and functions as such. Acting, feeling and thinking are not distinct and independent abilities: man's actions are motivated by his feelings (desires); that success or failure of his actions is reflected in accompanying and subsequent feelings; and his thinking **can** be used to direct his actions.

Since action and feeling (body and emotion) are so inter-related, it is reasonable to assume that if we utilize our cortical ability to direct our actions and to discipline our emotions the result will be a better integrated and more efficient organism. In other words, if we use our good judgment in our decisions we will usually be able to cope with our physical and social environment.

Conscious experience is always pleasant or unpleasant to some degree. These feelings of pleasantness and unpleasantness are closely related to an individual's likes or dislikes, and as such are a part of every psychological observation.

Psychology is most concerned with the traits that human beings possess in common. Everyone learns, acts, senses, perceives, remembers and thinks, although all people do not perform these functions equally well, or in exactly the same manner. Individual differences of behavior patterns, however, give each person his individuality, distinguish him from his fellows. Psychological studies take into consideration these differences, although the main interest is in the common tendencies and reactions possessed by all persons.

Personality

Personality is the sum total of an individual's habits of thought, feeling and action. Each person has a personality unique and distinct from that of every other person. The effect that one individual has on other individuals is his personality and it includes his attitudes, interests, likes and dislikes, aptitudes, and abilities. Personality is subject to change, depending on many factors, among which are the individual's inherited characteristics in reaction to his environment, his experiences, his education, his mode of living, the habits he has formed, his health, his vocation, his associates, his community, and many other factors in his physical and mental makeup and his surroundings.

Like all other phases of learning and study, the theories of personality have been many. It is interesting to briefly consider some· of these classifications of types.

Probably the first classification of personalities into types was done by Hippocrates in the fifth century B. C. He divided human temperaments into the sanguine, the melancholic, the choleric, and the phlegmatic, according to the dominance of certain bodily characteristics, which he designated as "humors."

Theophrastus, a pupil of Aristotle, described some

thirty types of persons, such as the penurious man, the boor, the flatterer, or the loquacious man.

Physiognomy, the interpretation of personality from physical features, particularly the face, began before Aristotle's time and revived with the Renaissance. While such claims have been made by some modern writers, most psychologists give no credence to this theory. In 1930 Donald G. Paterson summarized the case against physiognomy by stating: "Absolutely no evidence exists that shape of nose, mouth or ears, height of forehead, contour of skull, or any other feature has anything to do with personality." Gordon Allport says, "Our muscles, including those of the face, reflect life experiences to some extent, but our bony structures do not." Goring and Pearson measured features of 3,000 criminals and compared results with measurements of college students and army men. No differences were found between the physiognomies of criminals and of college men.

Some psychologists have divided people into two classificaitons of personality, the reasoning and the emotional. No definite or distinct line can be drawn here, for everyone is governed pretty much by both these factors, some being more subjective, some more objective.

Probably the best known type theory is Jung's introversion-extroversion classification. The introvert is preoccupied with his own impressions and psychological processes. He is content to live more to himself. The extrovert leans toward objective facts, is interested in activities of the outside world, enjoys more being with people, is socially-inclined. Jung said that everyone has tendencies toward both introversion and extroversion, though one or the other generally predominates.

Spranger, a German psychologist, classified people according to what values they believed most important. He noted six types: theoretical, economic, political, esthetic, social, and religious. He admitted that people do not fit exclusively into one or another category, but always show a combination of many or all of them.

The danger of thus typing people lies in our almost unfailing tendency to pigeonhole everybody in one category or another. Psychologists now regard types as extreme forms of personality traits.

Personality Traits

An individual's typical integrated way of reacting to situations, particularly to social situations, is his personality trait. This characteristic means one's consistent behavior rather than that which is temporary or occasional, and is another important point in psychological observations.

Personality habits are brought about chiefly by trial and error learning. The aggressive person is one who has found that he can satisfy his motives and gain his ends by direct action. The submissive person has hit upon the alternative solution of getting along with people by following the leadership of others. Childhood is the most important period for the acquisition of traits of personality, but modifications of greater or lesser degree continue throughout life.

Emotional development is especially important in the formation of traits of personality. Many children react to frustration by having tantrums of rage on some occasions, but most adults have learned not to resort to this overviolent emotional expression. If tantrums have been successful in getting an individual what he wants, and if circumstances have prevented the unlearning of this reaction, it may be carried into the adult years. Such a person must always have his own way, and is very unhappy if obstructed. Excessive fear, arising from many possible causes in childhood, may create a shy and overcautious personality. Too much pampering, or stimulation of the "love" type, often produces a person who expects others to give him special consideration and sympathy, and who therefore is oversensitive to slights and humiliations.

Although habit formation accounts for most of the variations in traits of personality, certain physiological factors also have some influence. An excessive secretion of the thyroid gland, for example, causes restlessness and overactivity. An undersecretion of this gland produces the opposite effects of lethargy, slowness and fatigability. A serious disturbance of the sugar metabolism of the body, as in diabetes, may cause depression and confusion. In individual cases it is necessary to consider these physiological disturbances in relation to personality. A given variation in personality may result from glandular factors in one case, and from purely psychological conditions of habit in another.

Traits of personality are usually rather permanent. Often, upon studying the history of an individual, one can detect the same typical responses of social reaction at the ages of five, twenty and fifty years. They remain fixed usually because they are learned so early in life and are practiced so much. They can be changed, however, by conscious effort and training. The earlier in life that such changes are attempted, the better and easier it is. For an adult to modify a personality trait is not impossible, but it is very difficult. Before attempting to make any change, the individual has to be clearly aware of his shortcomings, and must be strongly motivated to acquire a different characteristic. He must face the difficulty without making excuses for it and must not be afraid to try. In establishing new habits, one can not permit an exception to occur, but must be persistent in his attempts. When a habit is years in forming it takes time to change it.

One's basic "ego" makes it easy to interpret everything in terms of his own wishes and fears, and herein lies a danger. Our wishes and fears do **not** change facts; living is a continuous process of adjustment. Everything that is alive is constantly changing. Life means growth and growth implies change. **Everything is relative.** Even truth is relative.

To understand the relative nature of truth is the first step toward understanding life. Yesterday's heresies are today's truths; today's radicalism will be tomorrow's conservatism. In every realm new truth is discovered, violently resisted, and finally accepted, only to be superseded by a newer truth. The discoverer of new truths is persecuted, only to be recognized by future generations as the great discoverer that he is. Consider Socrates, Galileo, Pasteur, Darwin, and any number of other "pioneers."

Many things which were "true" yesterday are not so today. The world was flat and now it is spherical; the sun once stood still and now it moves; the physical world was once an inert mass and now its basic nature is movement; the insane were regarded as "possessed by devils" and now are treated as are the physically ill; illness and plagues were considered an expression of God's wrath over the actions of his recalcitrant children and now they are human problems which can and must be solved by human intelligence.

We smile indulgently over the ignorance, the superstitions of bygone days, but rarely wonder whether succeeding generations will find equally amusing our cherished beliefs which we "know" are "true."

It is natural to ask, "If facts are constantly changing, how can I know what is true?" Consider this: **Knowledge unapplied is worthless**. To admit the relative nature of truth is only the first step toward becoming intelligent. It is on this foundation that civilization itself is based. Concentrated thinking requires energy which many are loath to use.

Perhaps it is our desire for security that makes us resent change, that makes us cling so blindly and so stupidly to whatever is ours, whether material possessions or preconceived ideas. Stability is good if it is not carried to the extreme. At the opposite extreme from the "die-hard" is the impressionable person who is too easily swayed, and this is probably a worse condition than the first.

To admit that no truth is final and to be willing to abide by new discoveries does not mean that the partial truths that we do have are valueless. The best decisions are those that take into consideration all available pertinent facts.

The reader may wonder how the foregoing has any connection with a study of the psychology of grief.

The purpose of this discussion is to gain better understanding of the fundamentals of individual characteristics, as well as a better approach to the beginning
of a study of people.

A little philosophizing at this point might not be
amis. A fundamental truth to all persons is that **convictions are of value only when they result in action.**
Every experience has meaning and every experience
changes one's future, whether it be to the right or to
the left, so to speak. The meaning of life lies in our individual actions, which reveal what we think is necessary and fitting and desirable.

Emotional Stability

Another factor in human development that should
be understood in an introduction to a study of the psychology of grief, especially since it deals entirely with
emotions, is an understanding of emotional stability.
While there is a basic reaction by all normal persons to
specific emotions, yet there are many and varied de-
viations in the reactions of different individuals.

Emotional stability is an achievement, not an endowment; it is a skill perfected by practice; it is essential to maturity, effectiveness and happiness. Emotional stability is the essential element for developing
an integrated and satisfying life. By stability is not
meant fixity nor rigidity but rather a controlled and directed flexibility.

Extremes are dangerous; excess is eventually self-
defeating. Enjoy eating, but don't become a glutton;
be generous, but don't become a profligate; find pleasure in reading, but don't retreat from the world and
become a book-worm; take care of your health, but
don't pamper yourself, be thrifty, but don't be a miser;

be flexible, but don't be unmoored; be stable, but don't be immovable; take time to yourself, but don't become a recluse.

If we are going to study the emotions of people, and particularly grief, we should understand more about emotional stability.

Emotional stability is something infinitely more than external manner. There are wide racial and individual differences of temperament; so that to judge a particular person's degree of emotional stability demands far more knowledge than can be gleaned from observing his behavior or his speech. Of two persons equally frightened, one may scream and the other be "paralyzed" into silence; a grife-stricken person may be hysterical or he may be dry-eyed and tight-lipped; anger may express itself in stormy speech and violent gesticulation or in acidly and icily-quiet words. So far as the effect of emotion on the generation and perpetuation of symptoms is concerned, external manner is of little significance. The internal state of feeling is all-important.

So thoroughly does civilization inhibit spontaneous expression of emotion that we tend to discount all excessive manifestations as being "show" and, conversely, often mistake repression for absence or control of feeling. Children learn not to scream and kick when they do not get what they want. Prize fighters, whose sole intention is to injure each other, shake hands before they start. The defeated candidate congratulates his successful opponent. In our present state of society we rarely have the privilege of acting or speaking in accordance with our emotion of the moment. We mask our irritation, indifference, or boredom; we assume interest we do not feel; we urge tiresome guests to stay just a little longer, when we really wish they had left long ago; we muster a laugh for an old or inane joke; in other words, we try to make our manners conform with what we think is expected.

By emotional stability we mean direction and control of our emotional responses. While such actions hide the real inner feelings to a more or less degree, yet this is necessary in order to get along with others and to have a well-organized society. Emotionally unstable persons have fallen into the habit of overreacting to every stimulus. Emotional stability establishes and keeps control of situations, makes for a well-ordered world. It is the sign of intellectual progress.

Everyone on occasion is so overwhelmed by what he must face or endure that he would gladly turn his problems over to someone else. Sometimes he needs to do just that, for a person trained to handle certain situations can guide his path back to normalcy when he can again be on his own. A person who is ill places himself under the guidance of a physician. One in grief caused by death in the family depends on the mortician, as well as the clergy, in most cases. It is necessary, at least helpful, to have the trained guidance of these persons when these extremely difficult situations confront one.

The study of psychology by those planning to become funeral directors is essential as a means of helping persons who are emotionally upset and who must be readjusted to normal living. An understanding of psychology should enable the funeral director to help persons emotionally upset make the best possible adjustment to their bereavement.

CHAPTER II

HISTORICAL BACKGROUND

"In the Beginning"

In all scientific research the first step taken is to make a hypothesis or to "guess" at what might be true, then to proceed to prove or to disprove that premise. One of the first signs of human civilization was early man's curiosity about the things he did not understand. He wanted to learn the truth about those things unknown to him.

Because it is the natural inclination to fear that which we do not understand and can not control, primitive man's first "guesses" about such abstract sciences as religion, psychology, philosophy of living, were ridiculous superstitions. But they marked the beginning of such trends of thought, of development in these lines, and, since he had to start somewhere, who are we to ridicule him for these attempts? These early random thoughts or superstitions were beginnings of progress in scientific thinking. Perhaps our present attempts are only crude and awkward "guesses" that future generations will discard as entirely erroneous. But we are sincerely trying to learn the truth, and this was exactly the thing primitive man was doing when he formulated his theories that we now call superstitions.

Superstitions?

The earliest belief of what may be termed "mind" was that a ghost dwelt inside the body, making the body alive and conscious. At death this ghost or spirit permanently withdrew from the body; during sleep it wandered away temporarily. All bodily movement as well as sensation, feeling and thought were actuated by the ghost which was depicted as a "thin, unsubstantial human image, in its nature a sort of vapor, film, or shadow."

The ghost idea was also applied to everything in nature. Plants and animals had their spirits; rivers, ocean waves, thunder storms, all were possessed with these indwelling agents. There was no distinction between animate and inanimate objects. All nature was semi-personal.

This belief in a conscious "spirit" that leaves the body at death still persists in present-day religions. In fact, there are today organizations attracting sizeable groups of people that pretend to demonstrate the existence of "spirits from the other world." Man is still highly superstitious.

Why does this earliest concept of "mind" prevail so widely today over the world? The answer is not that man actually wants to believe in ghosts as such, but it concerns the natural peculiarities of human thinking. There are several characteristic traits in man's attempt to reason about himself and the world which easily lead to animistic notions. These traits, which reveal the fundamental nature of thought and the very framework of consciousness, may be considered as the confusion of self and environment, and as man's intense personal interest in himself.

In tracing the evolution of religious thinking we note this same tendency, that of ascribing human characteristics to the various deities created in men's minds. Probably few modern, present-day religious thinkers have evolved a "god" that has no human physical properties. The gods of all religions are gods that love and hate, that will bring destruction to the evil and reward the good, that will some day bring an end to this earthly travail. While these beliefs have always had an untold amount of influence in causing people to live good lives, and thus have inestimable value, yet they show the way man constructs the spiritual in the form of the physical. He does this because he is incapable of imagining something he has not seen or experienced with his physical body.

Man is still constructing and building. If we could not see weaknesses in present day thinking, then we would not be able to progress, to improve our sciences. This is the reason we can be reasonably sure that future generations will look upon our "truths" and "facts" of today in the same attitude that we look upon man's attempts of the past, as "crude beginnings of modern science."

The establishment of this conviction gives us our foundation upon which to build the proper mental attitude for further research. Psychology is in its infancy; it is a forming science. In its beginnings, psychology came out of philosophy. Since philosophy is always concerned with the principles or assumptions which lie behind different branches of human activity, all of the sciences are rooted in philosophy. Philosophy expresses the distinctive attitude which scientists take toward knowledge, and it involves all branches of learning. As each branch developed its own facts it branched out from the central trunk of research, philosophy.

With a philosophical approach in our study of psychology we shall be able to attain goals of understanding of which few have dreamed.

We know so little about human personalities, the mental reactions of people under diverse circumstances, their emotional makeup and response. If we will but approach this psychological study with the attitude that we have practically everything yet to learn, then we are ready to begin.

Primitive man had good reason to believe in his ghost theory, in thinking of his ghost as a sort of vapory substance contained within his body that left it at death and perhaps wandered away during sleep. On a cold morning he could see his breath. He did not understand the oxidation process. Vapor arising from fresh blood meant the same to him, for too much loss of blood meant death. Until recent centuries some of the most representative physiologists thought that the vapor from fresh, warm blood represented "animal spirits" or the vital agent of the body. The words "spirit" and "animism" are derived from older words meaning breath or vapor.

Dreams of dead persons, as well as dreams of one's self encountering strange adventures, formed good and logical reasons to early mankind for his "spirit" ideas. Since such beliefs persist today we have not yet progressed very far in this realm of thought.

In sickness and insanity the altered personal qualities of the individual appeared to be the intrusion of foreign ghosts. Noisy demonstrations to frighten the intruder are widely practiced among primitive tribes.

Trancelike states of hysteria have been considered

in every age to be a medium through which mystical revelations are received from visiting spirits.

If we can arrive at an impersonal, cautious method of study and research, then we are in the proper frame of mind to continue our approach to this vast field of emotional psychology. It is one of the last of many phases of psychological research to be attempted.

It is interesting to note that in primitive psychology mental states were localized. Some tribes placed the seat of intelligence in the ears, the seat of perseverance in the forehead where perspiration is most commonly seen. Strength they placed in the heart, vigor in the marrow of the bones, life in the blood. Conscience was in the breast, the heart or the throat. Some tribes placed feeling and will in the heart. Many located emotion in the lungs or breast. A man who felt elated said his breast was uplifted; one overcome by his emotions claimed his breast prevented him from speaking. One tribe indicated fear by the phrase, "the heart stands up." To soothe and comfort a person was to "knock down his heart." In disappointment the "heart was bent backward;" those about to die were "losing heart." A repentant man was one who "turned his heart around." Patience resided in the liver, conscience in the abdomen.

Thus we see the early beginning of scientific research in the realm of psychology, the first hypotheses or "guesses." It is only natural that certain expressions today contain elements of those early beliefs, for we still speak of a person as believing something "with all his heart."

Regarding death, the rule of early mankind was perhaps as follows: When the cause of death can be seen, such as attack by a tiger or a spear thrust, the death was considered natural; when no cause was obvious it was attributed to the working of evil magic or to the machinations of spirits.

Origin of Our Customs

Many of our present-day funeral customs originated in the early-day, primitive "spirit" beliefs. For example, early man always carried the dead body feet first so that it could not look back and see the spirit following it and thus permit this spirit to again inhabit the body. The custom of singing funeral songs is said to have its origin in weird chants and screams to drive away evil spirits.

Many peoples established the custom of removing the dead body from the house by way of a window or a hole in the roof so the spirit could not follow. Some peoples opened a window or placed a hole in the roof of the room in which the deceased died in order to enable the spirit to depart. One reason given for the establishment of the custom of covering bodies with earth was to prevent the spirit from finding the body and again inhabiting it.

Some races of people today still place food on the grave so the spirit can eat when it returns to visit the body. There are tribes who believe the spirit will not rest easy until all of the deceased's debts have been paid. The belief that the deceased's ghost will return and "haunt" those who might disobey the last wishes of the departed persists today among people even in our own land.

The superstition that the breaking of a mirror will

cause seven years of bad luck originated in the belief that the reflection in the mirror was the "spirit" or "ghost" of the person seeing the reflection. The number seven has for ages, since before there were written records, been considered a sacred number. Hence, the seven-day week with the seventh day as a Sabbath or a day of rest.

Another superstitious belief that a bird flying into a room means that someone within that house will die within a year results from the ancient belief that the bird, being able to fly to great heights, came from the spirit world—"heaven"—to carry away someone's soul.

There are countless other similar superstitions, many persisting today among our own people, that can be traced to this belief in active "spirits" or "ghosts." Such belief is older than civilization itself, goes back farther than written records reveal.

Such a long-established and deep-rooted conviction is going to continue in the minds of mankind, probably for all time. The spirit can never die, hence an afterlife, the only logical conclusion and a great comfort to all religious persons, which includes almost everyone.

Ancient Psychology

While other sciences have a more ancient origin, such as astronomy, mathematics, medicine, philosophy, the beginning of psychology can be said to be about 500 B. C. About that date Alcmaeon, a younger contemporary of Pythagoras, concluded that mental activity occurred in the brain rather than the heart as had been generally thought. His was the first scientific attempt to dissect human bodies. He is said to have brought forth evidence to show that the brain is connected with the sense organs.

Anaxagoras (460 B. C.), one of the early "pluralists," gave the first hint at a separation of mind and body by using the term "nous" to designate "thought-stuff."

Democritus (420 B. C.) discussed the five senses and gave definite expression to an ancient distinction between the kinds of mental activity which are located in different parts of the body; he said that thinking is located in the brain, anger in the heart, and appetite in the liver.

Thus we see in this period the beginning of a distinction of the mental from the physical. This was the first materialistic trend.

Socrates (424 B. C.) urged a careful self-criticism of inner experience and presented the motto, "Know thyself." His pupil, Plato (387 B. C.) established the notion of dualism by teaching that man should free the Psyche (mental activity) from the adulteration of the material flesh. He emphasized the unifying function of the mind. Mental activity, he claimed, occurs in four ascending steps: conjecture, belief, comprehension and reason. His teachings predominated in Europe during the first twelve centuries of the Christian era.

Aristotle (335 B. C.), a student of Plato and tutor of Alexander the Great, intimately connected his treatment of psychology with his study of biology. To him, mind is a part of nature.

Following the death of Alexander the Great (323 B. C.) the political power of Greece declined and the trend of thought changed. Two schools of thought then arose in Athens: the Epicureans (306 B. C.) and the Stoics (308 B. C.) Epicurus emphasized the attainment of serenity and tranquility of mind, while Zeno "the Stoic" emphasized a state of indifference. Early Christianity denounced the Epicurian doctrine but favored the Stoic ethics which flourished until 200 A. D.

Another line of thought, an escape from the perplexities of life, was taught by Pyrrho (365-275 B. C.), known as skepticism. It was an attitude of complete distrust and rejection of any facts or principles. Pyrrho taught that the correct attitude of mind is to withhold all judgment and to restrain all action. His favorite method of answering questions was to keep silent and merely shake his finger. This influence was short lived, however, because Greece was incorporated into the Roman Empire in 146 B. C.

Cicero (75 B. C) translated a great deal of the Greek sciences into Latin. He believed in the certainty of consciousness regarding moral and religious ideas which he claimed are known in common to all men. These common innate ideas he called conscience.

Religious Period

There next followed a period in which attention was given mostly to religion, to the neglect of advancement in psychological research. Two men in this period merit mention. Philo (39 A. D.) combined Hebrew theism with Greek rationalism. He taught that reason is immortal and is the breath of God. Saint Paul (67 A. D.) gave the doctrine of inner experience a psychological form in his classification of soul, mind and body.

Saint Augustine (306 A. D.) made the first use of introspection as a definite method of investigation.

For more than a century there was nothing contributed to psychology worth mentioning. Europe's population was shifting, the early Christian Catholic Church controlled thinking, the crusades were promoted to drive the Mohammedans from Europe and Asia Minor, with the result that scientific progress was stifled.

Martin Luther in 1518 initiated the Protestant movement. Being weary of scholastic compromises, he urged that philosophical arguments be separated from simple religious faith.

Period of Discovery

A variety of events during the 16th century affected the trend of psychology. Columbus' discovery of a new race of people in a new world (1492), Magellan's circumnavigation of the globe (1519) demonstrated that a unanimous opinion believing the earth was flat was wrong, Copernicus (1543) disproved the belief of astronomy that the earth was the center of the universe, Gallileo's invention of the telescope (1609), Newton's revelation of gravity (1687), Harvey's discovery (1628) of the circulation of the blood from the heart as a muscular organ,—all these events were upsetting the established teachings and beliefs held by scholars previously.

Renaissance Period

During the period of the Renaissance such men as Bacon (1620), Descartes (1630), Hobbes (1651) and others contributed to the advancement of psychological thinking, particularly by discovering more about emotions.

Period of Enlightenment

From the period of the Renaissance we come to the period of the Enlightenment, when were developed three principal lines of thought: empiricism, rationalism and naturalism. Locke (1690), Spinoza (1665), Hume (1739) and Kant (1781) were the best known contributors during this period, each adding his reflections to the store of knowledge already gained by those preceding.

From here until the beginning of modern psychology we can see in studying the works of the scientists of the time the trend toward the revaluation of mental processes. The anatomists and physiologists were learning more about the nervous system and the brain. Scientific knowledge was approaching the point where an enlightened study of psychology could really begin.

Naturalism

There also developed a naturalistic trend of thought in Europe, which included such men as Voltaire, Rousseau and others. This school of thought claimed the human body is wholly a machine. The mind was characterized by spontaneous reaction set off by sensory disturbance. It was Gall (1809) who climaxed this trend of thought with the doctrine of "phrenology," the reading of the bumps of the skull to denote mental development of an individual. Mental activity caused localized enlargements, bumps on the cranium.

In the latter part of this Enlightenment Period

there were various psychological theories proposed. Brown (1820) brought forth the idea of "suggestion," that ideas themselves act to arouse other ideas. Previously it was believed that ideas were passive. Herbart (1816) introduced the "subconscious" idea. Comte (1840) introduced the term "sociology." He treated the mind as a social rather than as a physiological product.

Beginning of Modern Thought

The character of modern psychology has been determined largely by the demands of the other sciences. Physics, astronomy, and medicine have each encountered the need for a definite knowledge of the precision of human judgments and sensory discrimination. The insistence of these problems turned the main course of psychological interest away from the philosophical aspects to a distinctly experimental approach.

Haller (1759) introduced modern physiology by furnishing experimental demonstrations of many facts which previously had been treated only as theoretical propositions. He established the validity of the hypothesis that irritability is a specific, immanent property in muscle tissue, that sensibility is a property common to nervous tissue and to tissue supplied by nerves. He established these facts by actual experiments and dissections. His notions of the brain were not progressive, however. He believed that memory is correlated with the cerebral convolutions.

Wyatt (1750) helped to disprove the old notion that the brain is the source of all nerve impulses by showing that sensory-motor reflexes may take place in isolated segments of the spinal cord.

Pinel (1801) is credited as being the first to investigate the problems of insanity from a scientific viewpoint. He regarded insanity as a medical problem and engaged in a thorough reform of the cruelly oppressive treatment of the insane patients who were still looked upon as being possessed with demons. His care of the patients consisted of physical treatment only.

Bell (1911) confirmed the distinction between sensory and motor nerves.

Other psychologists of this time discovered and established such facts as sensory discriminations, speed reactions to stimuli in individuals, specialized sections in the brain, and mathematical calculations measuring stimulus sensation intensity.

Evolutionary Approach

Darwin (1859) introduced the genetic approach to psychological problems in his argument that man evolved from lower animal forms. He suggested that many human expressions of emotion are continuations of actions useful in the animal. e. g., the sneer is a continuation of the animal's preparation to bite. In comparing the mental powers of man and lower animals he showed similar evidence of imitation, curiosity, imagination and even of reason. The genetic approach was soon extended to the study of animal, child and racial psychology.

Spencer (1855) combined the evolutionary doctrine with associationism. His evolutionary formula accounted for every change in the universe. In the field of psychology Spencer claimed that the first undifferentiated units of the mind are little else than "nervous shocks." Individual ideas by continually being associated with each other are forming general ideas or concepts. Thus, ideas grow and develop as the physical body has grown and developed. They also evolve.

Galton (1869), a cousin of Darwin, conducted many studies of heredity, attempting to prove a tendency for superior intelligence, or genius, to run in families, as shown by the biographies of famous men. He established the law of "filial regression," that the characteristics of offspring regress toward the average characteristics of family stock. His theory of "eugenics" aimed at the elimination of unfit humans and sought a general improvement of the race. His outstanding contribution to psychology was his demonstration of "individual differences" between humans. His tests were the forerunners of the modern intelligence tests.

First Experimental Laboratory

Wundt established psychology as a separate science. He established the first experimental laboratory of psychology in Leipzig in 1879, thus ushuring in modern, scientific psychology. His first psychological work was concerned with sense perceptions and with meanings attached to sensations. In the study of attention Wundt found that in the simultaneous presentation of two stimuli one will be perceived before the other if it has been expected and attention has been directed toward it.

Ribot (1885), another experimental psychologist, classified the unstable emotional states, which are often called hysterical, as "emotional infantilism."

Other discoveries during this period had to do with physical manifestations of emotion, such as blushing, frowning, nervous tapping of fingers and walking about when under stress, and others dealing with joy, sorrow and other states.

Beginning of American Contribution

The beginning of American contribution to psychology was in the late 19th century. The study along scientific lines was becoming quite well established in Europe by this time.

In 1890 William James described mental life as a biological function of adjustment between impressions made upon the body and the reactions of the body upon the world. He gave to emotional expressions a significance, as opposed to the former belief that such states were chaotic conditions. He believed that ideas always lead to action. It was James who introduced the first laboratory work in psychology in America.

During this period there was advancement made in the treatment of insanity. Hypnotism was explained as the result of suggestion. Evidence was presented against the inheritance of acquired characteristics.

Freud (1895) introduced his teachings, including his belief that sex was the most fundamental drive in everyone's life, that emotional drives that are denied an outlet are the cause of dreams, and developed the method of treatment known as psychoanalysis.

Hall (1904) expanded the scope of genetic psychology. He made extensive use of the theory that in the individual, in his development before and after birth, are reenacted all the steps of evolution beginning with the remotest primitive ancestral organisms. This is called the "recapitulation" theory. For example, the gill-like formation which occurs during a period of prenatal development recapitulates the fish stage of ancestral evolution, and the manner in which a very young infant clings to a horizontal support rehearses the arboreal behavior of his ape-like ancestors. During the period of adolescence in every individual's life when childhood habits are being discarded and· adult manners are not yet acquired the person depends largely upon inherited racial habits, resulting in an awkward physical condition.

Adler (1907) made self-assertion the basic impulse in human conduct. Disappointment and failure produce an "inferiority complex" for which the individual tries to compensate by exaggerations in behavior, such as delusions of grandeur.

Jung (1910) classed personalities in two sorts: "introverts," who constantly evaluate everything in terms of their own feelings, and "extroverts," whose thoughts and actions constantly reflect external influences.

Watson (1913), a behaviorist, made his most valuable contribution to psychology in the study of infant behavior. He found three distinct patterns of emotional response. These are fear, characterized by trembling; rage, characterized by rigidity; and love, characterized by cooing and smiling. From these basic emotions the many complexities of feelings in later life are derived through the process of conditioned response.

Through the study of infants it has been learned that there are two inherent fears in every individual, the fear of a loud noise and the fear of falling.

The majority of psychologists use both the behavioristic and the introspective methods, according to their needs. Each method has yielded fundamental facts. Introspection has served as a constant aid to the study of the senses; the observation of behavior has disclosed important principles, such as the conditioned reflex.

In view of evidence presented on both sides concerning the parts played by heredity and environment in characteristics of individuals, it can be stated that "heredity and environment are not antithetical, nor can they expediently be separated."

While there are many psychologists not mentioned in this brief review who have made valuable contributions to the science, space does not permit their mention. The few mentioned herein are most of the best known leaders insofar as our own particular phase of interest is concerned. This brief mention of these few men gives an idea of the steps taken in the development of psychological thought from the earliest records to the present.

CHAPTER III

THE NERVOUS SYSTEM AND GLANDS

THE NERVOUS SYSTEM

In order to better understand bodily emotions and the various reactions to stimuli it is necessary to have an acquaintance with the nervous system and its anatomical structure.

The entire human body, organs and consciousness, are harmoniously integrated by the immense network of the nerves and nerve centers. Just as the capillaries go to every cell in the body to nourish the entire organism so do the nerves go to every portion of the body to report the condition of every bit of tissue, membrane, and all substances in the body makeup. These nerves report pain whenever any portion of the body is not normal, or has been injured or upset in any way. It is the nervous system that controls the behavior of every organ in the body and keeps the entire system functioning under all conditions.

The structure and function of the nervous system can be compared to our modern telephone service. The sensory nerves report sensations from all parts of the body to the central switchboard, the spinal cord and brain. From this central point the commands are sent to the muscles of the body where action might be needed to preserve the safety of the structure. An individual places his finger on a hot object accidentally and before he realizes what is happening he quickly pulls his finger away. The nerve impulse traveling at the rate of one hundred meters per second seems instantaneous in this quick response.

It is the ability to react to stimuli that preserves living organisms. The well-being of the entire organism is dependent upon the well-being of each and every part of that organism.

The nervous system is the very center of the entire physical makeup and the developed, mature nervous system of the human is very complex. Every living organism has some sort of a nervous system that at least gives it the sensations of pain or unpleasantness; all living things are capable of reaction to stimuli, but it is the human organism that is placed at the peak of complexity and development. Man is the most highly evolved.

In the comparative anatomy of the nervous system we find even in primitive forms that nerve fibers and cell bodies have a tendency to cluster together. In all higher animal forms, not only is this superiority of the head ganglion or brain preserved, but it may also be said that the complexity in structure of this organ is directly related to the complexity of behavior.

Primitive Development

The primitive central nervous system as is found in fish is shaped like a tube, one end of which has various thickenings, each one of which is connected with a particular sense organ. In the higher animals is found a "brain stem," the various parts of which correspond anatomically to the thickenings of the neural tube representing the fish brain. There are no cerebral hemispheres in lower forms of life, although in the fish brain there is the beginning of division.

As the cerebral hemispheres develop progressively in the amphibia, reptiles, birds and mammals, they take over many of the functions of the parts of the brain stem. Thus we find the shifting of functions from the lower centers to the cerebral hemisphere as the brains of lower are compared with higher forms of life in the order of evolution.

From the study of prematurely born babies and of living embryos and fetuses surgically removed from the womb in emergency operations, plus the study of movies of fetuses, much has been learned of human development before normal birth.

Embryonic Development

In embryonic development, the nervous system begins to form in the fourth week of life, at about the same time the heart can be recognized as such, and immediately before the food canal can be noticed. A thickened oval plate forms in the embryonic disc, called the neural plate. This rolls up into a tube in the middle of what will be the embryo's back. The front end of this tube will later develop into the brain and the back part will become the spinal cord. At this four week period of development, the embryo is only a tenth of an inch long, but it already shows the ground plan of a human being.

At eight and one-half weeks it can be stimulated to reflex movement of its head and arms by tickling with a hair. At twelve weeks the nervous system is becoming developed to the extent that it will arch its back and open its mouth when its back is tickled.

Development continues so that at the end of 28 weeks it may live if prematurely delivered. When the embryo is 36 weeks of age it can cry lustily, sleeps soundly, notices human faces, looks pleased when caressed, is soothed by handling. At the end of 40 weeks it is a full-term baby and is completely developed in every way.

It is believed that, through this information on the growth and development of babies before birth, much of what has been considered learning actually has nothing to do with education, but is a natural, inevitable process of mental growth, progressing by predetermined stages independent of the enviornment.

Whatever an animal is, the kind of existence it leads is determined by the nervous system with which it is provided. The simple, unspecialized bodily organization of the amoeba creates for it a simple world and a simple life. The more highly specialized nervous system of higher animals and birds opens up a more complex world, resulting in a more varied existence. For man, whose nervous organization is most complex and most highly specialized, the. world is most extensive and differentiated, his life most varied.

Three Systems

The entire nervous system of a vertebrate animal has three principal parts: (1) the **central nervous system**, which consists of the brain and the spinal cord, and controls all of the activities of the organism; (2) the **peripheral nervous system**, which comprises the nerves that branch out from the central nervous system, and which carries impulses to and from every part of the body; and (3) the **autonomic nervous system**, which controls automatic behavior such as heart action.

The **central nervous system** is of the greatest significance to psychology, because its two most important parts, most prominent divisions, are the brain and spinal cord, the seat of control for the whole body. The brain can be divided functionally into two sections, the "lower" brain centers that control the simpler and more essential life processes, and the "higher" brain centers that are concerned with the more complex experiences and the more skillful adjustments, located in the **cerebrum**.

Like all other living parts of the body, the nervous system is composed entirely of cells. The structural unit of the nervous system is the **Neuron,** a highly specialized irritable cell that can conduct an impulse throughout its length and transmit it to another nerve cell or to a muscle or gland. The neuron is made up of the cell body and two kinds of branches, dendrites and the axon. An impulse runs in one direction only, from the dendrites to the axon.

There are three general classes of neurons, **sensory, association,** and **motor.** The sensory neurons carry impulses from the sense receptors into the central nervous system; the motor neurons convey the neural currents outward from the cord or brain to the effector muscles and glands; the association neurons connect the sensory to the motor neurons, and convey the neural currents from the sensory to the motor fibers, and also from one part of the spinal cord or brain to another.

When a neuron is stimulated, an electrochemical change occurs along its fiber. This disturbance passes rapidly along the fiber as a wave of excitation. An impulse travels about 100 meters per second in man.

Responses are graduated according to the strength of their stimuli. A brighter light causes a more intense visual experience, and a more severe pin prick causes a more vigorous withdrawal of the hand. A stronger stimulus brings more fibers into action and raises the frequency of impulses that the fibers transmit. The strength of a response therefore is determined by the number of impulses per second that reach an effector or organ of response, a muscle or gland.

A nerve is a bundle of nerve fibers. The nerve is not a conducting unit itself, but a collection of relatively independent units that have adjacent origins or destinations in the body. A nerve may be compared to a telephone cable which contains a large number of separate conducting wires. The numbers of fibers in a single nerve vary greatly. There are approximately a half million in the optic nerve of the human eye. The fibers that make up a nerve range up to several feet in length.

Some of the great nerves issue directly from the brain, and are known as **cranial nerves**, while others that arise from the spinal cord are called **spinal nerves**.

Both cranial and spinal nerves occur in pairs, since the nervous system is completely symmetrical.

There are twelve pairs of cranial nerves that pass directly from the brain chiefly to sense organs and muscles located in the head and neck. One pair goes to the receptors for smell located in the nose, another pair to the eyes, and another pair to the organs of hearing and equilibrium in the ear. The sense of taste from the tongue is also transmitted to the brain by the fibers of cranial nerves. Other cranial nerves carry motor impulses to the muscles of the eyes, jaws, tongue, face and neck. One pair of cranial nerves, the **Vagus**, goes down into the trunk and serves the heart, lungs and digestive organs. The normal functions of breathing and digestion are regulated largely by impulses that pass down the vagus nerves from lower brain centers.

The thirty-one pairs of spinal nerves, having their origin in the spinal cord, emerge between the segments of the vertebral column, one nerve of each pair from the right and one from the left. They are named from the region from which they originate. There are 8 cervical pairs in the neck region, 12 thoracic pairs back of the chest, 5 lumbar pairs in the lower back, and 5 sacral and one coccygeal pair in the terminal region. The spinal nerves convey motor impulses to the muscles of the trunk and limbs, and bring in sensory impulses from the receptors located in the skin, the muscles and the visceral organs.

The connecting and integrating functions of the central nervous system are performed at all levels of its structure. In general, the most elementary and fundamental coordinations may be made by the lower centers in the spinal cord and in the inferior parts of the brain. The more complex activities are integrated by the higher nerve centers of the cerebrum.

The spinal cord has three principal functions. First, it is a primary connecting center for some very simple bodily movements known as reflexes. Second, it is an integrating mechanism that coordinates the movements of large groups of muscles and of whole parts of the body. Third, it is a connecting cable that conducts impulses up to the brain centers and down from them.

With a very few exceptions, all sensory and motor neurons cross over to the opposite side of the nervous system before reaching the final connecting center. In general, the left side of the nervous system controls the right side of the body, and vice versa.

At its upper end, the spinal cord merges with the more complex structure of the brain. The human brain may be described as a series of parts which assume successively more complex functions from the bottom to the top.

While it is not necessary to go into any detailed study of the functions of the several divisions of the brain, a brief mention of them will be made. A bulbous enlargement at the top of the spinal cord is the **medulla oblongata,** through which large bundles of nerve fibers pass from the spinal cord to the higher brain centers. Destruction of the medulla results in immediate death, for in it are connecting centers which control some of the most vital functions, such as respiration and heart beat. The **cerebellum** is a large structure lying above and behind the medulla, whose function is the control of muscular tone, bodily equilibrium and posture. The **pons** ("bridge") encircles the upper part of the medulla. It consists chiefly of bands of fibers that connect the cerebrum with the cerebellum. The **mid-brain,** four small nodules above the pons, contain sensory reflex centers, such as jumping at a loud sound, co-ordination of the eyes. The **thalamus,** two eggshaped lobes, one on each side just above the mid-brain, have sensory and motor functions which serve as protective elements of sensation, such as pain and temperature. Injury to it causes sensations to be excessively painful.

In man, the fore-brain is represented by the highly developed **cerebral hemispheres** which occupy about two-thirds of the cranial cavity and form about one-half of the total weight of the entire brain. The **cerebrum** is divided into lobes: the **frontal lobe** or fore part, the **parietal lobe** or middle part, and the **occipital lobe** or rear portion. Functionally, the **cerebrum** is divided into the surface "gray matter" or **cerebral cortex**, and the internal "white matter." The **cortex** is the most significant part of the entire nervous system with respect to complicated and adaptive behavior. Here, in a layer of nerve cells and dendrites about three millimeters in thickness, are made the connections for the most specialized activities of the organism. The cortex is the essential center that operates in all instances of problem solving, voluntary action, thinking and imagining. To perform these functions the cortex has to be elaborately connected both internally within itself and externally with all other parts of the nervous system. This function is performed by the innumerable fibers that form the "white matter.'

Some parts of the cortex are connected to the sense organs and are essential to the functions of conscious sensation. Each of the senses of smell, vision, taste and hearing has its particular portion of the cerebrum which is as much a part of that sense as the organ itself. The complex mental activities of learning, reasoning, thinking and imagining are not localized, but represent the efficient interrelation of many centers by the combined activity of all the nervous system. Men can, therefore, be reeducated after brain damage resulting in loss of skills of action.

While the brain is a unitary organ in its most complex functions, although an infinitely complicated one, the simple vital functions are carried out by fixed neural circuits that are not capable of much modification.

The **autonomic nervous system** regulates the action of the viscera, or the internal organs, that serve to maintain the body and to reproduce the species.

The **sympathetic nerves** also supply all the principal visceral organs. These nerves have as their function the acceleration of the heart beat, deepening of respiration, slowing or stopping of digestion, such as when an emergency arises in the life of the organism and great exertion is needed for its safety, when fatigue sets in, or when a strong emotional state such as fear or anger is aroused. The sympathetic innervation may cause perspiration, erection of body hairs ("goose flesh') and the dilation or contraction of the small blood vessels. These effects are present during an emotional reaction.

While the sympathetic nervous system prepares all parts of the body to meet emotional stress when such action is needed, the cranial and sacral nerves of the autonomic system keep all parts of the body functioning as nearly normally as is possible, thus preserving the life of the organism during and after emotional stress.

GLANDS

The glands of the body play an important part in the emotional life of the individual. The glandular secretions provide bodily maintenance in normal bodily activity and prepare the body to meet emergencies in times of stress. Since glandular activities are under direct control of the nervous system they will be briefly considered in this chapter. The direct results of glandular activity will be treated in the chapter under emotions.

All glands of the body may be classified in accordance with the nature of the discharge of their chemical secretions. Those glands that have an external outlet, and consequently discharge their secretions either on the surface of the body or into some body cavity, are classified as **duct** glands. Those glands that have no external outlet, but discharge their secretions either directly or indirectly into the blood stream, are classified as **ductless** or **endocrine** glands. A few glands of the body pour out both external and internal secretions.

Duct Glands

The duct glands are concerned with essential processes of bodily maintenance. The salivary glands help to dissolve food substances placed in the mouth. The gastric and intestinal glands, along with the liver and pancreas, function in the process of digestion. The sweat and sebaceous glands serve to remove waste products form the body. The tear glands supply the lubricating liquid of the eye. The reproductive glands provide for the continuance of the species, through function as duct glands.

Ductless Glands

The ductless or endocrine glands pour their secretions, directly or indirectly, into the blood stream, where they are carried to all parts of the body. These secretions are of two kinds: (1) those which exert an excitatory influence on behavior, called **hormones**; (2) those that have an inhibitory effect on behavior, called **chalones**, or inhibitory hormones, which act to slacken bodily activity.

The **thyroid** gland, which lies just below the Adam's apple, secretes a powerful hormone called thyroxin. If there is an undersecretion of the thyroid gland in the child, bodily growth is arrested, the reproductive organs fail to develop, mental growth retarded. In adults, a deficient thyroid secretion, or a complete loss of it, produces a dry skin, brittle falling hair, increased weight, and general inactivity. Such a person is frequently emotionally depressed, lacks interest in things around him, and is retarded in his thinking. If the gland oversecretes, it causes fast heart action, general nervousness, irritability, and a number of other similar symptoms.

The **parathyroid** glands consist of four small bodies about the size of peas which lie in the thyroid, although they probably have nothing to do with the activity of the thyroid. A malfunctioning of these glands causes muscular tremors, cramps, spasm, and often maniacal excitement. The complete removal of these glands will cause death.

The **adrenal** glands are above and in contact with the kidneys. Each gland has two different structures, the cortex or outer part, and the medulla or central portion. The adrenal cortex secretes a hormone, "cortin," which has influence on all body cells. When the cortex fails to function, the individual becomes restless and irritable and shows general bodily fatigue. The secretion of the adrenal medulla is called "adrenalin" and plays a great part in emotional excitement, which we shall consider in detail in the chapter on emotions.

The **pituitary** gland lies underneath the brain. It is divided into a posterior and anterior lobe. A hormone from the anterior lobe promotes the growth of the bones and bodily tissues. Over-secretion of this hormone results in excessive bodily growth. Other pituitary hormones exercise a stimulating effect upon the development of the sex glands and secondary characteristics on the function of the thyroid gland, and on the fat, carbohydrate and water metabolism of the body.

The **Islands of Langerhans**, which in humans are embedded in the pancreas, produce insulin, a hormone concerned in the utilization of carbohydrates by the body tissues. A lack of insulin in the body causes diabetes.

The endocrine function of the **reproductive** or **sex** glands brings about a development of secondary sexual characteristics, such as the distribution of hair on the body and change in voice. Removal of the sex glands in the male during youth results in abnormalities such as a high-pitched voice, a beardless face and lack of regular masculine aggressive qualities. Removal of the ovaries in the female often causes tendencies toward masculinity.

The **liver**, important as both duct and endocrine, transforms waste products in the blood and regulates the sugar content of the blood, in its endocrine functions.

The **pineal** body, located in the head near the brain, and the **thymus**, located in the chest, function most actively in childhood and tend to atrophy after puberty.

CHAPTER IV

LEARNING AND MEMORY

Their Importance

The problem of learning and memory is one of the most important in the whole field of psychology and in the whole field of human relations and behavior. All human behavior involves learning and memory in some form or other. We have learned from a stimulus that an incident has occurred and we remember this fact because of the impression the happening has made upon the brain. Some future occasion may arouse this incident in the mind, and this we call memory. The ability to recall requires a proper stimulus.

The importance of learning and memory in our everyday human contacts is evidenced by the fact that we must frequently recall the names of those we have previously contacted and we must remember certain things that must be done each day. We must so impress these facts on our minds that recall will be forthcoming at the proper time and place. Many people berate themselves for the apparent inability to remember others' names, and this is probably the most common complaint in this field of human endeavor.

When an impression has been made in the gray matter of one's brain why should it be so difficult to recall the incident making this imprint at the instant it is needed? Why are we not able to remember as we wish? There are several factors responsible for this.

The basis of all learning consists of some animal tissue which is plastic enough to be affected by changes impressed upon it and yet sufficiently retentive to keep a record of such influences. The higher developed organisms of life are much better able to record experiences and to again recall them under the proper stimulus than are so-called lower forms in the evolutionary scale.

The Effect of Learning

Once an individual has learned something, that individual is a different person, his entire future is altered. This change is constantly and continually going on throughout the entire life of every living organism. The more highly developed the organism the more things it is able to learn and to retain and recall. Therefore, higher forms of life are undergoing more frequent changes than are the lower or less developed forms.

The ability to modify behavior through experience is a characteristic of all living beings. The sparrow, when reared with canaries, learns to sing like a canary. The rat, when placed in a maze, learns to find its way to the food. Even the lowly earthworm learns which way it must crawl to avoid the sandpaper and electric shock of its "T-maze" experimental device. This capacity to learn is of highest importance to all living beings. The greater an animal's ability to learn, the greater its chance for survival.

It is by virtue of his complex brain that man surpasses all other animals both in the speed and the range of his learning. It is to this capacity more than any other that he owes his dominant position in the world.

Studying is deliberate application to a new task. Learning is a process that goes on continuously, embracing all activity that makes later behavior different from what it would otherwise have been.

The Learning Process

The learning process follows certain definite laws. It involves, first of all, the presence of a learning situation. This arises when a need manifests itself with sufficient strength to force the organism to action. A "trial and error" period usually follows when the organism explores various possibilities, testing different avenues of approach and making many responses inadequate to the successful realization of the goal. After a sufficient number of trials, the so-called "random" or "faulty" in what the organism does becomes eliminated, and responses are thus narrowed down to those which are most effective in satisfying the goal.

Every reaction that an individual makes causes some slight change in his nervous system. Conduction pathways are modified in the process of learning so that some neural circuits become more likely to conduct and others less likely to do so. It is thus easy to understand why the individual is constantly changing; he is not quite the same individual after he has learned something than he was before he learned it.

The age and experience of the individual make considerable difference in learning. Youth has few established habits to break in learning new ones, while age has the benefit of experience in which he can associate new material with something he has already learned. Both have advantages and disadvantages. Youth will probably make more errors in learning, while age will make fewer changes in habits and behavior. Youth finds it easy to adopt new ideas and motor habits because it has few old ones at variance with the new.

Age finds it necessary to break established routine and habit in order to adopt the new. Old habits persevere. The older individual, however, finds many of his established habits useful. The fruitful period in learning is between the time an individual matures and the time senility sets in.

Laws of Learning

While it is not the purpose of this study to go into anything like exhaustive detail, there will be here presented a few of the conditions which favor or hinder learning. These conditions are commonly referred to as laws. This study will consider external conditions, for it would be impossible to observe directly all the neuromuscular changes that occur during learning, such as the growth of neurons, the modification of the connections between neurons, changes in conductivity of nerve impulses and other possible structural and functional alterations.

Before any learning can occur there must be a desire on the part of the individual to reach a certain goal, to accomplish a specified task. There must be **motivation**. One cannot do well what one does reluctantly, so no learning occurs without a motivating force. There must be a motivation to memorize or to master a problem. One must want something.

The Law of Frequency holds that, of two neural pathways, the one which has functioned more often will, other things being equal, offer less resistance to the subsequent passage of nervous impulse. This law is embodied in the statement that "practice makes perfect"; that repetition leads to perfection.

The more often material is repeated the more

lasting will be its impression and the more easily it is to recall. **Repetition** is the one certain road to recall. There is no more definite method of learning than that of frequent repetition.

Of two neural pathways, the one which has functioned longer will, other things being equal, offer less resistance to the subsequent passage of nervous impulse. This is the **Law of Duration.** If material is to be remembered it must be gone over continuously. One remembers the names of friends whom he sees frequently and he does not forget them ever if he sees them throughout the years. Absence of recall causes one to forget; at least he will forget first those things which have not been experienced or recalled for a long time.

Other things being equal, the neural pathway which has functioned last will offer less resistance to the subsequent passage of a nervous impulse, which gives us the **Law of Recency.** However, this "law" probably has more exceptions than any other. Old persons, for example, remember much more vividly the incidents which happened in their youth than someting that happened only yesterday, or even an hour ago. To the normal person, however, with all his faculties functioning properly, the more recent the incident the better it is remembered.

The Law of Vividness holds that the more vivid of two experiences will be retained longer than the less vivid. For example, a house that is painted a bright green or a bright red or blue will be remembered longer than one painted a conservative color. It is the contrast to the ordinary that causes it to be more easily recalled.

The Law of Primacy affirms that the first experience of a type is likely to be remembered longer than subsequent ones. A doctor's first patient will no doubt linger in his memory longer than any subsequent patients. A lawyer's first case in court he will always remember, even though he may try hundreds of cases during his life. A mortician will probably never forget the first funeral service he conducts by himself. The first experience in any line of endeavor is the most impressive because it is special. Most of the following patients or cases or services become ordinary and routine and make no particularly lasting impression. The "first" requires more concentration, more effort.

The individual will learn more quickly if the rewards or punishments are more intense, so we have the **Law of Intensity**. A child who has been burned will remember to keep a safe distance from the fire. A hungry rat will learn more quickly the intricacies of a maze leading to food than will a rat that is not so hungry. In the business or professional world, an individual will be more alert to conditions and will benefit to a greater extent if competition is keen than the same individual would if he had no competition. He is more intense in his efforts. His response is more highly motivated.

The Law of Organization states that learning is more rapid when material is organized into meaningful relations. To learn a list of meaningless, disconnected words is much more difficult than learning a story that has contiguity and sequence, where one word and one paragraph suggests the one that is to follow. That material well understood is more easily learned has practical implications that need not be enlarged upon.

If a stimulus in a new situation utilizes a previously learned response, then the one act of learning assists the other and we have the **Law of Facilitation**. For example, a knowledge of Latin makes it easier to learn Spanish because so many Spanish words are derived from Latin words and are similar. If, on the other hand, the learning of one thing has an adverse effect upon some other learned act, this is called the **Law of Interference**. It is usually difficult for an experienced public speaker, being used to formulate the words in his statement as he speaks, to memorize and deliver material "word perfect."

It is obvious that repetition is required for most learning. **The Law of Exercise** means just this. In memorizing a poem or learning to perform an act, the more times it is repeated the more nearly perfect an individual becomes in the performance. This law depends on other laws, however. There must be attention given to the performance if any good is to result. A child may write a word correctly a hundred times and be thinking about the ball game he is missing during this time and at the end of the period he will not be able to spell the word correctly without a copy before him.

In associative learning there is a **Law of Contiguity**, which means that the associated events must fall within a certain time interval in order for the association to occur.

The Law of Effect means that a response leading to a satisfying result will be learned willingly, while a response leading to an annoying result will not. A perch and a minnow were placed in a tank of water with a glass plate between. After repeatedly striking at the minnow and bumping his nose on the barrier the perch finally desisted and left the minnow alone even after the partition was removed. A pupil who dislikes poetry will have a difficult time learning to recite a poem and will make no attempt to remember it longer than is absolutely necessary.

Economical Methods of Learning

Many students spend much time on assignments that could be learned in much less time if better methods of study were applied. The first requirement in learning is **Concentration**. Anything that prevents or hinders concentration must be avoided. Concentration means nothing more than giving strict **attention** to the matter under study.

One of the first things to be guarded against is distraction of attention, either through daydreaming of more interesting topics, or because of noisy and fatiguing environments. Distraction increases fatigue, even though output does not decrease. The worker musters more effort to overcome the disturbing tendencies. This condition is detrimental to efficiency. Where concentration of effort and attention is desired, distracting forces should be eliminated in so far as possible. One way to keep a· dog from chasing cats is to keep the cats away from him. In a student's room, a pile of love letters on the table, several issues of popular magazines, a phonograph or a radio, or a plate of cookies or apples certainly do not accelerate his studying.

One brilliant and accomplished professor has described the difference between his college roommate and himself in studying. His roommate spent so much time getting everything ready for study, a comfortable chair, a reading stand to hold books, lounging robe and slippers, and many other incidentals, that when he finally got down to studying he went to sleep. This professor, immediately upon entering the room, opened his books and started studying in the quickest arrangement, regardless of comfort, and was through his lessons in a short time because he concentrated on the lessons themselves, not the environment. Leisurely arrangements for study are not conducive to its progress, but speed of concentration is.

Irregular disturbances, such as noises, are more detrimental to efficiency than are regular ones, because the sudden sounds tend to set off a fear reaction, while the regular hum or drone leads to negative adaptation on the part of the listners.

After eliminating distraction the matter of motivation must be kept constantly in mind. If there is little or no motivating force there will be little accomplished. Studying for an examination which is to be held in a short time will stimulate a student to speedy concentration, while if the examination is a week away he will not apply himself so readily.

In considering the most economical methods of learning there are possibly four methods that should be given consideration.

(1) **Distribute the Trials**. The more the trials are distributed in point of time, up to certain limits, the faster will be the learning in actual time spent. If one has only a short time in which to learn, then the trials cannot be properly spaced for the most efficiency. The less time available for learning the more trials necessary for perfection.

(2) **The Whole versus the Part Method**. The whole method of memorizing is usually superior to the part method. Instead of stopping with smaller units, such as stanzas and paragraphs, the entire piece should be read through from start to finish. In this way the attention is uniformly distributed throughout the material. Too, the individual parts memorized in the part method may become difficult for the learner to place in their proper place in the whole piece. Instead of going on to the next he is inclined to return to the first line of each part, with difficulty of recalling them in sequence.

Some material may be actually too long to learn as a whole, in which case it must be broken into parts. The whole method seems longer to the learner in the time it takes, and if the time is really short he may have to break it into parts, but when he is able to reproduce the material learned by the whole method he can usually reproduce all of it more easily and with less effort. In the time spent, the whole method is more efficient.

(3) **Learn One Subject at a Time**. For the quick development of habits, it is well to concentrate on one habit at a time. If too many things are attempted at once there is confusion and loss of coordination and efficiency. Monotony may tend to appear in using the single track method, so the motivation must be kept strong. For actual time spent in learning, the single item method produces the result in less time spent.

(4) **Active versus Passive Learning**. Active learning shortens the learning time and renders more serviceable the material acquired. A student can read material a few times and have it learned if he reads it

with the **intention** to learn it. If he is just reading the material in a casual way, with no effort to memorize it, it would require many times the amount of reading before he really learned it. In ritualistic work, for example, a member of an organization may hear the officers give the same material time after time and be able to catch any error instantly. But unless this member concentrated on the ritual material with the intent to actually learn it himself, he could never get up and recite it.

Overlearning and frequent repetitions after the material is fully memorized also lead to greater retention.

Some Facts in Memory Improvement

Bad memory, or rather lack of good memory, is the result of faulty learning. **Memory Improvement,** therefore, **really amounts to improving our methods of learning.**

Motivation is the first step in remembering, whether it be names or other items. A stimulus is required in order to bring to mind something that has been learned. This stimulus may be an association or it may be direct.

For all practical purposes, the one thing that is complained of the most, probably, is the seeming inability to remember others' names and to recall them instantly on sight. When an introduction is made and the name spoken, the name should always be repeated in order to assist in impressing it for future recall. Names which are spoken are much more easily remembered. Frequent repetition of the name will further impress it upon the mind.

If a name can be written down and seen it is usually more easily remembered, for 87% of our impressions are obtained through our sense of vision, while hearing gives us only about 7%. Written material is more easily and quickly learned than is material that is listened to only.

Mere passage of time does not cause forgetting. Probably all forgetting is due to interference. Tests have been taken on material learned just before going to sleep for the night. Upon awakening eight hours later, much of the material had been remembered. Material learned shortly after arising in the morning was tested for retention eight hours later in the day and found much of it forgotten. There had been no interference during the sleeping hours, but much interference during the daily activities. Upon further testing it was found that most forgotten material learned just before going to sleep at night was forgotten in the first hour; practically nothing was forgotten between the second and eighth hour of sleep. Whatever interference there was evidently occured in the process of going to sleep.

Pleasant experiences are more easily remembered than are the unpleasant. Tests have shown this to be true. College students have been asked to record all the experiences they could remember during a vacation period. Several weeks later, without any warnings, they were again to list their experiences during this same period. Of the pleasant memories 53% were retained, while only 40% of the unpleasant were recalled. In common experience this is found to be true. To most persons, childhood is remembered as a joyous experience because pleasures are remembered better than the sorrows. After a vacation trip taken, the pleasant occurrences stand out more vividly than the unpleasant. Of course, it is pleasing to recall happy events, while painful experiences are usually not repeated but are inhibited. There are exceptions to this, of course, but it is found to be the general rule.

Learning How to Remember

It is possible to improve the ability to remember in some degree by learning how to use efficient methods for acquiring and recalling. Training in **Methods** of remembering yields far better results than does mere practice in memorizing. There are several principles of effective memorizing and aid in remembering, among which are:

1. Learning by wholes. While both the whole and the part methods have advantages, efficiency favors the whole method.

2. The use of self-recitation. The student goes over the material, then without looking at it he attempts to recite it. Then he reads it again to catch his errors.

3. The use of rhythm and grouping. This is helpful if the learner uses a little ingenuity in applying the system.

4. Attention to meaning. If the meaning of material is understood it is much more easily learned than merely learning the words. The meaning should be understood first of all.

5. Alertness and concentration. This is more than anything else the result of habit. Outside factors are a strong influence, as previously described, but the

primary motive to alertness and concentration lies within the individual himself and the learning habits he has formed.

6. The use of associative clues for recall. The more associations from familiar material that can be used in learning and recalling new material the more easily it is accomplished.

A simple example is the difference in difficulty for an English-speaking person in learning, for example, Spanish on the one hand and, on the other hand, some Slavic language like Russian. Most words in Spanish or French or German have cognates, related origins, that the English-speaking person can use as a frame of reference. But since these cognates are almost entirely missing in Russian, learning the language becomes extraordinarily difficult.

7. "Set" Learning and Retention. "Set" performance means that if some specified exercise or routine or situation immediately precedes the attempt to learn, then such learning will be aided. Likewise, memory will be aided if this same "set" is experienced prior to desired recall of facts learned previously.

It should be possible to increase the rate of learning in a new situation by inducing in the subject an adequate "set" to perform immediately before he begins to learn.

In practical life, for example, sitting at his office desk aids a businessman to perform routine acts in his business schedule, brings to his mind certain things he has done and is yet to do during the course of his daily business routine. Entrance of the student into the school library should induce study; the presence of other students studying lends to the atmosphere of study of books. Such atmosphere will call to mind the lessons to be learned. Facts learned in the classroom should be more easily recalled in that classroom.

The "set" is an aid in learning and memory. It should be used as much as possible.

A careful application of these methods will yield large dividends in the improved efficiency of the functions of acquiring and recalling.

Conclusion

Memory improvement really amounts to improvement in the learning process. The laws of learning, coupled with motivation, attention, and the intention to remember, are the chief instruments through which an individual increases the memories available. After an impression has been made upon the synapses, this impression tends to remain. A part of memory improvement is concerned with making vivid impressions on the nervous system. The linking of one idea with numerous associated memories renders it more available to recall.

It is the ability to learn and to remember that makes for all progress, that enables an individual to think. Were there no memory there would be no change, no improvement. This ability to compare past experiences with present conditions and project these into future possibilities is responsible for all order and organization in life and for all stability.

CHAPTER V

EMOTION

Emotion Defined

Emotions are intensified feelings. An emotion is an urge to action. Emotions involve stirred-up states in an individual, such as anger, fear, grief, joy, hate, love, sorrow, shame, all involved in meeting emergency situations with emergency responses. To the individual experiencing them they are states of intense inner excitement. To the onlooker they appear as muscular and glandular distubances that may take many outward forms, as tears, laughter, clenched fists, accelerated breathing, scowling, blushing, screaming, tembling, etc. To the psychologist these emotions imply drastic internal readjustments that prepare the organism for swift action based on impulse.

The organic upheaval that occurs during emotion is related to the requirements of a primitive environment. In such an environment it usually was a matter of life and death for the organism to be able to struggle, fight or run away with a maximum of effectiveness. In modern society, struggling, fighting, or running away is often impracticable, but the internal changes generated in emotion and the impulses that accompany these changes are still the same as those originally effective for emergencies in a primitive world. When under the sway of emotion, man shows himself to be the product of a long span of evolutionary development.

Emotions are aroused by emergencies, the unusual happenings as contrasted with routine occurrences. The acts known as emotional behavior are those that are caused by experiences of the individual that really upset usual patterns of response and change the usual normal functioning of the organism. Literally, the word 'emotion' comes from two Latin words which mean 'to move out of.' This moving out of the normal, routine state of feeling, then, is to agitate, to disturb.

Emotion is that modification of the body by which the power in action of the body is increased or diminished, aided or restrained, to accomplish an end which is in the final analysis the well-being and preservation of the bodily organism.

Historical Approach

Emotions were recognized as such and were studied apart from ordinary reactions as early as 350 B. C. when Aristotle analyzed several concrete emotions, among them being anger, hate, fear, courage, envy and joy. He admitted that some emotions arise through mere disturbances of the body and cannot be brought under the control of the intellect. He subordinated the appetitive life of feeling to thought and reason. Nevertheless, he gives sensation and emotion a more important role than did Plato, by admitting the body may at times get out of control in strong emotion. In all such instances he maintains that reason must struggle to overcome the body and attain the end which it approves.

The Stoics had as their guiding principle the ideal of escaping from the control of emotions.

The ideal of the Epicurean school was the reverse of the Stoic in one sense, by making happiness the measure of human conduct.

Descartes in the early 17th century mentioned six

primary emotions: admiration (wonder), love, hate, desire, joy and sadness.

Spinoza in the middle 17th century gives three primary emotions: joy, sadness and desire. Joy corresponds to bodily well-being and progresses toward an end; sadness to bodily ill-being or to being thwarted in progress. Desire adds to the others a slightly conscious awareness of seeking an end. All the other emotions are derived from these by the addition of different ideas.

Other psychologists in the 18th and 19th centuries gradually became more cognizant of the bodily reactions to emotional experiences.

Wundt, in the middle 19th century, wrote about bodily changes during emotions. Actions are derived from emotions, for no act or no decision is made unless some emotion be present.

Darwin shows that man's emotional expressions are survivals of movements that were once useful to the animal series.

Ribot taught that instinct and emotion are different phases of the same fundamental physiological process. Emotions are the awareness of the vague fundamental drives or appetites which have remained at a low level of evolution and so are accompanied by only vague consciousness.

Modern Teachings

Modern psychology shows a wide divergence of opinion regarding emotions. A few of these will be mentioned briefly.

The common popular belief has always been that the emotions produce the bodily changes, that these changes are the expressions of emotions. This has also been the view of the early experimental psychologists.

A theory just the reverse of this is known as the James-Lange Theory, named for its two authors. This theory is that the bodily changes occur first and the impulses sent to the brain render us conscious of the occurrences; i. e. we are sad because we cry; we are afraid because we tremble; etc.

To the **behaviorist** the bodily changes **are** the emotions.

Some psychologists hold that the bodily and emotional changes run a parallel course, side by side. The one happens at the same time as the other.

Some psychologists do not regard emotion as ever the simple setting off of a given pattern of behavior by specific stimulation. Instead, they see emotion as arising when behavior is blocked. This is described as the arrest of tendency, a reflex action which cannot terminate as it would. Examples of this would be hunger or thirst.

Some psychologists attack the specific pattern theory of emotional behavior and maintain that emotional behavior is not patterned at all but is rather a disorganization of the behavior with which the individual is trying to meet the situation. To them an emotion is a disorganized response, largely visceral, resulting from the lack of an effective adjustment. Subjects studied to reach this conclusion included murderers immediately after apprehension, and students awaiting exclusion from university study already begun.

Others, taking the opposite view, maintain that in all emotional behavior there is always some element of organized activity, either reflexive response (crying, smiling, startled expression) or some goal-oriented activity (running from danger, striking an enemy, pouring water on fire)—a reaction of the organism against its environment.

While psychologists are still groping for a genuine understanding of feelings and emotions, we can assume this much, (1) that emotional urges are inherited pattern reactions involving extensive visceral behavior and intense feelings and (2) that emotional behavior changes as the individual gains in intelligence and becomes more nearly mature.

Emotional Response

In primitive life and in early childhood, vigorous responses almost always are a part of emotion. Since primitive man was forced by circumstances to react physically to his emotional feelings in order to survive, these identical responsive urges have been inherited down through the ages. The small child fights or flees or has a tantrum, in response to his emotions, the normal inherited tendencies. Present day adults have learned to prevent these overt expressions, but the internal changes are less easily controlled and may occur even when the individual does not want to become agitated.

Such intense emotional response has a disorganizing effect on other processes of behavior and thinking. Hence, the aroused person is less skillful, less careful and less capable of making fine discriminations. Thus a ball player can easily become excited and "lose his head" and cause the team to lose the game. Under excitement he is not able to play skillfully, not able to think clearly. In escaping from a burning building a person may do all sorts of unexplainable things. On the whole, however, present day civilized man has learned to rationalize his actions to a much greater extent than did primitive man, or than a child is able to do. Experience has taught him to do this.

Ontogeny recapitulates phylogeny. The progress of the individual from childhood to adulthood parallels the progress of the human race from its early primitive state to its present level of behavior. Civilization is a learned pattern of behavior, and it is quite easy for man to permit his emotional urges to remove that veneer, as is witnessed in war.

Uninhibited emotional response can perhaps be best studied in the behavior of infants, with acquired and learned patterns of behavior being acquired as the individual matures.

The newborn infant is a bundle of reflexes in whom the first sign of emotion is excitement. This may turn into fear, anger or some other specific emotional state. Behavior of the infant is largely mass action, not precise or specific. Specific behavior develops with growth, and especially in response to the infant's social environment. During excitement in the young infant the arm and hand muscles are tensed, the legs make jerky, kicking movements, the eyes are opened as if gazing into the distance and the upper lid is arched.

The original emotions persist as the infant develops, and more and more specific emotions become differentiated out of the earlier patterns. The two-year-old, for example, still exhibits general excitement, distress and delight; but in addition to these basic emotions he has by this age acquired several more specific emotional responses, as fear, disgust, anger, jealousy, joy, elation, affection.

As the individual advances from infancy to adult life the characteristics of his emotional life change radically. When his emotional development reaches a certain stage we say that he is emotionally mature. For example, the infant is intolerant of discomfort and thwarting. The older child is more tolerant. As the individual becomes older there is a decrease in the frequency and degree of emotional upset. The capacity to endure pain and to face danger with fortitude is a criterion of emotional maturity. The adult is less overt in his emotional manifestations.

Emotional Patterns

Watson gives us three primary emotional patterns: rage, fear, love.

Bridge's genetic theory of emotion says emotional development consists of: (1) decreasing frequency of intense emotional response; (2) progressive transfer of emotional responses to situations which are socially approved and determined by experience; (3) gradual change in the nature of overt emotional responses in accordance with training and social pressure. Social and emotional responses are intimately related.

Harper places all emotion in two groups: (1) tenseness which may grow into excitement (anger, courage, fear, confusion); (2) relaxation which may grow into depression (sorrow, remorse, satisfaction).

Either tenseness-excitement or relaxation-depression is always found in any emotion.

An emotion is a very general phenomenon in the sense that it seems to be diffused throughout the body and to be connected with every aspect of behavior.

Through processes of learning, individuals develop patterns of differentiated emotional behavior that are designated by such terms as fear, grief, disgust, anger, jealousy, excitement, joy, love. Emotional habits are determined in large measure by the cultural environment of the individual. There are both similarities and differences in the emotional behavior of different peoples, different races of peoples, as between Scandinavian, Chinese, Slavs, Latins, etc.

Basic Emotions

Fear is the most fundamental of all emotions, for in a newborn baby are found two basic fears, a sudden, loud noise and a dropping sensation. Fear, the most typical of emotional reactions, is a state of nonadjustment and often results in a **phobia**. The sufferer from a phobia feels a strong fear of some harmless situation. He admits it is foolish but can not control it. Common phobias are fear of high places, closed rooms, crowds, and animals. Phobias are conditioned fear reactions, caused by a forgotten experience that caused it originally. To cure a phobia the individual must make a new response to the fearful stimulus.

Grief is derived from distress, and is dependent upon an intellectual development sufficient to understand the loss or injury of loved ones. The emotion of grief will be studied in detail in a later chapter.

Sympathy is related to grief and is socially conditioned.

Disgust is also social in origin, depending largely on learned habits of custom.

Anger is elicited by an interference with activity or desire. People are aroused to anger by obstacles they cannot overcome. The angry man usually reveals his state by certain expressions of emotion that are attenuated remnants of the more complete primitive response; i. e., his face flushes or turns pale, his eyes partly close, his nostrils distend, his teeth are bared, his fists clench, his whole body becomes tense. A "terrible temper" is due to the individual having learned no better way of responding to frustration, especially by those "given in to." Undisciplined children usually develop such tempers.

Jealousy is chronic anger, as is **resentment**.

Hate is a compound of anger and fear.

Embarrassment is a mild, angry confusion resulting from an awareness of inadequacy.

Delight and **joy** are stirred up and excited feelings.

Love produces an unsettled state.

Emotional Control

There is no question but that certain individuals experience emotion more readily than others. Hereditary factors may here come into play. Some individuals may come from more placid stock than others; they may be slower to respond to stimulation and therefore less easily thrown off their balance or excited. This does not mean, however, that people who do not show emotion do not experience any, for it should be borne in mind that present day civilized society places great virtue on the ability to inhibit most outward signs of emotions felt. The environment in which an individual is placed determines to quite a large extent, also, his reaction to emotional stimuli.

Some persons can control emotional behavior better than others. The "even-tempered" (poised) person is one who uses cortical control in dealing with emotion-arousing stimuli, or whose habitual emotional behavior has been formed by directed cortical activity.

Emotional control, although one of the greatest developments of personality, is not the absence of all emotional expression. An individual should be able to adjust himself to the situation. Humanity is rich in modes of feeling; in possibilities of being interesting through emotional adjustment.

Emotional Response

The emotional tone is fixed to quite a large degree, although environment may modify or change an individual's emotional responses; experience does change them. A coward is almost always a coward, even though he covers up this feeling with an air of arrogance, particularly with weaker persons and those occupying inferior social or economic positions. There are instances where a coward has become a brave man by means of experience and environment. Environment often is the deciding factor in changing emotional reactions. A child in danger may cause a man to brave a danger from which he would otherwise run.

Bodily activity is an exceedingly important outlet of emotional energy. A stirred-up bodily state tends to disappear or be converted into a more satisfactory form through bodily activity. James said: "When you have grief, do something worth while that you probably would not otherwise have done." Carr says: "An emotion gradually subsides and finally disappears as the organism begins to respond to the situation in an orderly fashion." The athlete is nervous just before a game or a race, but this emotional excitement soon subsides as physical activity gets under way. An actor may have "stage fright" until the play starts and he is on the stage speaking and acting, then the nervousness leaves.

To a certain degree every emotion finds some bodily expression: in trembling, blushing, turning pale, etc. To a large degree these reactions are hereditary.

When feelings are fanned into emotions, the organism experiences strong impulses to action. Such impulses are helpful in a primitive environment. But in civilized society they are often an encumbrance, since society requires that we curb most of them. If emotion is strong, their blocking is one of the most painful of all experiences, fraught with serious internal consequences. Thus, a criminal recently executed with instruments attached to his body, was reported to have registered a pulse of 160, rising to almost 300 at the moment of death (as against a normal of 70). As a result of such an upheaval he would have developed serious internal trouble had he been reprieved and lived. Likewise, excessive irritations of a business day may result in the complete stoppage of digestion and in a harmful increase in blood pressure, for the organic effects of emotion linger for some hours after the emotion has passed.

It is for this reason that violent emotion often

leaves a person exhausted and sometimes even makes one sick; for this reason, too, that such states should, insofar as possible, be resisted before they get out of hand. Letting oneself get annoyed or irritated at the slightest provocation is an indulgence which may easily prove very costly in the end.

The doctrine of human development from a subhuman ancestry has done much to unravel the complex nature of man. Corroborating this discovery is the fact that the total human body, composed of countless numbers of cells, acts and reacts no different from the manner which is characteristic of the simplest form of animal life, even down to that of our microscopic progenitor, the amoeba. All animals, single or multicellular, are capable of ingesting and excreting food; of moving toward pleasure and away from pain or danger; of being stimulated or depressed and of reproduction. Two major points here become increasingly apparent: (1) that the motivating, actuating drives are, for amoeba and all forms of life up to man, essentially identical, and (2) that man has an infinitely greater technique of control over his environment than does the unicellular form of life or those many forms all along the evolutionary scale between the amoeba and man; a much more complex mechanism with which to satisfy his needs; and, as a consequence, potentially much more freedom. In actuality, "civilization" has so elaborated and complicated his fundamental desires that his problems are much more multiform and acute and his chances of frustration much more numerous. The lowest form of life has exactly the same potentialities as has the highest form, man, except in a matter of degree. As man "decides" matters of movement in his "mind," so must the amoeba "decide." He must find food and escape danger, swim away from pain and toward pleasure. He must also reproduce. Fundamentally, does man do more?

The faculty of deciding, in its primitive state, is in reality merely doing that which is conducive to the best development of the organism. The amoeba, if confronted simultaneously by a pleasurable and by a dangerous stimulus, does exactly what any higher form of life, even man, would do. It will attempt to escape from the danger toward the pleasant.

The "emotion" is merely the state of the organism as it is going through the motions towards pleasure or away from danger. Emotion is, therefore, a state of the organism while it is responding to a stimulus. The emotion is a response involving three aspects: visceral activity, skeletal (overt) behavior, and conscious activity. The only difference existing between lower and higher forms of life is the degree or complicated state of the response or activity. Higher forms of life have a more complicated nervous system that reaches a high state of development and complexity in the brain. The brain is a station of delay in its function, the purpose being to test the best possible type of response to a stimulus. Only to the extent that animals can delay their responses are they capable of thinking. Lowest forms of life respond without any apparent delay.

There are many surface manifestations of excitement. The contraction of blood vessels with resulting pallor, the pouring out of "cold sweat," the stopping of saliva flow so that the "tongue cleaves to the roof of the mouth," the dilation of the pupils, the rising of the hairs, the rapid beating of the heart, the hurried respiration, the trembling and twitching of the muscles, especially those about the lips,—all these bodily changes are well recognized accompaniments of pain and great emotional disturbance, such as horror, anger, and deep disgust. But these disturbances of the even routine of life, which have been commonly noted, are mainly superficial and therefore readily observable. The internal organs of the body are all affected by emotional stimuli, which do not reveal such disturbances of action but which attend states of intense feeling.

When a person is disturbed his total organism is involved and its normal functioning is upset. The whole human body reacts to the person's real feelings, to his mental state. To be healthy is to be free from anxiety. Emotional stress seriously limits the adjustability of the organism in the sense of its ability to maintain a stable equilibrium. It is not an overstatement to say that fully fifty percent of the problems of the acute stages of an illness and seventy-five percent of the difficulties of convalescence have their primary origin not in the body, but in the mind of the patient. Our emotional states as definitely determine the well-being of our bodies as they reflect it.

Continuous irritability, constant fretting and worrying, states of fear and apprehension and their counterparts, states of dislike and hate all combine to produce a constant state of high blood pressure. When this state remains high for a long period of time, permanent changes occur in the blood vessels so that the condition becomes fixed and the blood pressure cannot be reduced. In some individuals, however, the reverse action is true, and low blood pressure instead of high is produced.

Organic Responses to Emotion

The heart is the first organ affected in emotional disturbance, in its rapid beating. The next portion of the body to be thrown off its normal course is the digestive system. W. B. Cannon, authority on bodily changes, writes: "An emotional disturbance affecting the alimentary canal is capable of starting a vicious circle; the stagnant food, unprotected by abundant juice, naturally undergoes bacterial fermentation, with the formation of gases and irritant decomposition products. These in turn may produce mild inflammation or be absorbed as substances disturbing to metabolism, and thus affect the mental state. . . Just as feelings of comfort and peace of mind are fundamental to normal digestion, so discomfort and mental discord may be fundamental to disturbed digestion."

Since the sympathetic nervous system controls the various glands that are so active in cases of emotional emergencies, the cortex has no direct control over the functions of the viscera. It is impossible, therefore, to try, by merely thinking about it, to check a racing heart or to lower a high blood pressure, or to renew the activities of an inhibited digestive system by a coldly reasoned demand for different behavior. The occasion for worries, anxieties, conflicts, hatreds, resentments, and other forms of fear and anger, which affect the thalamic centers, must be removed, and it is the cortex that is concerned with the outer world. A person can often avoid the circumstances which arouse fear or rage and their attendant visceral turmoil.

The "ordeal of rice" as employed in India was a practical utilization of the knowledge that excitement is capable of inhibiting the salivary flow. When several persons were suspected of crime, the consecrated rice was given to them all to chew, and after a short time it was spit out upon the leaf of the sacred fig tree. If any one ejected it dry, that was taken as proof that fear of being discovered had stopped the secretion, and consequently he was judged guilty.

What has long been recognized as true of the secretion of saliva has been proved true also of the secretion of the gastric and all digestive juices. The mere sight or smell of food may start the pouring out of digestive juices. The proper starting of the digestive process is conditioned by the satisfactions of the palate and a pleasant frame of mind. The conditions favorable to proper digestion are wholly abolished when unpleasant feelings such as vexation and worry and anxiety, or great emotions such as anger and fear, are allowed to prevail.

We have previously studied the chief functions of each division of the autonomic nervous system: The cranial division is the upbuilder and restorer of the organic reserves, the sacral is the servant of racial continuity, and the sympathetic is the preserver of the individual. Interruptions of the nutritional process for the sake of self-preservation through defense or attack (action of the sympathetic division, abolishing those influences to the cranial division which are favorable to proper digestion and nutrition) can be only temporary. If the interruption were prolonged there might be serious danger to the vigor of the organism from failure to replenish the exhausted stores.

Any high degree of excitement in the central nervous system, whether felt as anger, terror, pain, anxiety, joy, grief or deep disgust, is likely to break over into the threshold of the sympathetic division and disturb the functions of all the organs which that division innervates.

The adrenal glands are stimulated to extra secretion under any excitement. At such times the glands pour out an excess of adrenalin into the circulating blood stream. The purposive nature of this reaction is to safeguard the organism, the body, to preserve its welfare. Adrenalin injected into the blood causes liberation of sugar from the liver into the blood stream; it relaxes the smooth muscles of the bronchioles; it acts as an antidote for muscular fatigue; it alters the distribution of the blood in the body, driving it from the abdominal viscera into the heart, lungs, central nervous system and limbs; it renders more rapid the coagulation of the blood. Every one of these visceral changes is directly serviceable in making the organism more effective in the violent display of energy which strong emotions involve,—that is, in the physical display of energy.

To be specific, if a man is angered by another man, his first impulse is to strike the man angering him. This is an outlet which nature provides for the emotion of anger. Adrenalin injected into the blood in this instance would enable this angered man to endure an unusual amount of physical exertion. A man alone in the woods, unarmed, sees a wild animal, say a man-eating tiger. His first impulse is to escape. He may attempt to run or to climb a tree, anything that enters his mind first to escape. Nature immediately stimulates the adrenal glands which, by the pouring of an excess amount of adrenalin into the blood stream, gives this man what seems to be superhuman endurance, in his fright. He might be able to jump over an obstacle that ordinarily would be impossible for him to scale. He will be able to run several times the distance he could run under ordinary conditions, or he could climb a tree that would be impossible without the stress of the present situation. Under the influence of adrenalin and other secretions called out from the ductless glands by the major emotions, the organism's physiological state is so changed that it can do things (and endure things) which it could not do when such secretions are absent. This is the real evidence for the assumption that the emotions furnish the "drive" for many forms of activity.

Briefly, the principal specific bodily changes experienced in emotions are:

> Excessive adrenalin produced, causing:
> > Rapid heart action
> > More oxygen into the blood
> > Refreshed muscles
> > Hastened blood coagulation
> > Loss of appetite
> > Blood to head and limbs
> > Rapid and deep breathing
> > Excessive perspiration ("cold sweat")

Emotional physical responses are, as we have seen, survivals from an age of primitive conditions in life. They prepared the body for fighting or flight, for extreme physical exertion which was necessary for survival.

Emotional Reactions Suppressed and Controlled

Under civilized conditions of life these emotional upsets are detrimental because they prevent clear thinking and carefully planned action. An unhealthy body condition results because there is no adequate physical outlet. A man watching the stock market ticker, for example, may sit and watch his fortunes being wiped out and physically experience extreme emotional upset, the same as primitive man being attacked by a physical enemy. In both circumstances the body would be prepared for extreme physical exertion. But the man watching the stock market ticker can do nothing but sit motionless, giving no outlet of any nature to his pent-up emotions. Much of this will make a sick man of him. Hence, athletic clubs, golf and the many sports that give physical exercise are beneficial. In addition to building up the muscle tone these exercises provide an outlet for the emotions built up under "civilized" conditions.

Most men today do not strike one another upon becoming angry, but take some other means of "obtaining justice" or "getting even" or they allow the situation to pass without any visible reaction at all. The emotion provided by nature is experienced just the same. Through civilization man has trained himself through acquired skill and knowledge to adopt less violent measures in meeting situations that disturb his well-being. Adaptation, or adaptive reaction, may be defined as being any response which is appropriate to the situation presented by the stimulus. It is the purpose of adaptive reaction to render the well-being of the bodily organism more secure by easier and more dependable methods than were used by more primitive or less civilized man.

It is because man has learned a less violent and a better way to act that he does not immediately perform the act dictated by the primitive impulse within him.

We have seen that emotions produce acute physical reactions. The physical act of blushing is a response to the emotion of embarrassment; trembling, palpitations and increased sweat secretions accompanying fear; disgust may lead to nausea; shuddering and gooseflesh may be produced by horror or sudden fright as well as by cold; the act of "breathing easier" comes after a dangerous or anxious period is past; "taking a load off the chest" is the feeling after expressing pent-up thoughts. These experiences are commonplace to all.

As civilization progresses, under the progress of cortical (gray matter) development, it is evident that the physical expressions of emotions no longer play the part in life that they did ages ago. The devising of weapons that could kill at a distance lessened the number of personal hand-to-hand encounters. We talk ourselves out of the many situations that would otherwise result in personal combat. Courts of law take the place of physical encounters. Emotional reactions of the violent type have been largely replaced by cortical action in adaptive behavior. Better control is assumed over physical reactions.

However, these so-called "civilized" reactions to emotions are only on the surface. Down deep the reactions are the same; every gland and every nerve perform the same functions for modern man that they performed for primitive man, for our civilized state is very recent when compared with the millions of years man's physical organism has been developing. Internal physical reaction to emotion is still violent. Psychiatrists have long contended that emotions can lead to incapacitating or even fatal physical illness. A sick mind can cause a sick body. Moral disgust readily expresses itself in physical nausea; a fatigued spirit makes an exhausted physique; a hated task or endurance, for which one has no desire, causes loss of appetite. Nervousness in all its forms usually springs from nonphysical sources.

Emotional Disorders

A great deal was discovered during the two great world wars concerning emotional disturbances. Particularly was World War II a war of nerves. Cases of supposed heart trouble were discovered to be "cardiac neurosis," an emotional rather than an organic cause. It has been estimated that between forty and fifty per cent of all arm disability cases are of psychosomatic origin. This high percentage was due partly to the emotional stress and strain of war, partly to better recognition of psychosomatic diseases, partly to the notable triumphs of medicine over bacterial infections. As the infections have declined, the relative proportion of psychosomatic ailments has increased.

There is no way of estimating accurately the number of people in the total population who are afflicted with psychosomatic illnesses. In addition to the commonly accepted ailments of peptic ulcer (stomach ulcer), mucous colitis and other gastrointestinal disorders being classed as psychosomatic, this is also believed to be the cause in some cases, of such disorders as bronchial asthma, hay fever, hypertension (high blood pressure), arthritis, heart ailments, rheumatic disease, diabetes mellitus, the common cold and the various skin conditions such as hives, warts and allergic reactions. In addition, many other diseases caused by bacteria are prolonged and recovery hindered and even prevented because of the mental attitude of the patient. Even in cases of obesity, caused by overeating, the act of over-eating is in many instances an act whereby the gour-mand compensates for some inner deprivation or frustration.

Many times accidents are directly traceable to ner-vous conditions of emotional origin. Many people seem to constantly have mishaps of one kind or another, and seem to have a predisposition to accidents. One promi-nent psychiatrist has estimated that from eighty to ninety percent of all accidents are not due to defective machinery or to any physical or mental defect or to a lack of skill, but to an emotional factor in the person.

In such instances, if the person can find the source of the emotional difficulty and as a result can change his job, change his surroundings and atmosphere, or otherwise alter the external circumstances which bother him, his troubles will likely disappear. However, most cases are not as simple as this remedy may seem to indicate.

Intelligent Approach Essential

In reference to the things learned during World War II about intense emotions, let us consider related instances, common occurrences of normal service men. For example, the soldiers on the convoys experienced emotions resulting from extreme danger without being able to utilize any physical activity whatsoever. The navy operated the guns during the attacks from the air and the soldiers aboard all freight ships could only sit idly by and "sweat it out" when bombs or shells started flying. One soldier was asked how he liked coming in on these boats. He replied that he didn't like it any too well. "The trouble is," he said, "that you feel so darned defenseless. If you could just man a gun and shoot back it wouldn't be so bad."

From a large number of detailed questionnaires filled out by U. S. fighting men in World War II, some general conclusions were reached. Among these are that fear is normal. Most of them said the oftener they went into action the less they were afraid. Fear always has bodily symptoms, as pounding heart and rapid pulse, muscular tenseness, a "sinking feeling in the stomach," dry mouth, clammy hands.

Most of the men thought fear should be openly discussed before battle. Knowing he is not the only one afraid makes a man a better soldier. Most of them believed the signs of fear should be suppressed in battle. They felt a soldier should get rid of his shame of fear, concentrate in battle on his task, replace his fear by other forces, such as belief in aims or ideals of the war, in the leadership, training and material. Regimental pride had a great power against fear.

This observation of the effect of fear and the feeling of fear on the service men in the most violent of all wars gives us a better insight into the emotions experienced and the control of them, thus lessening their damage to the physical organism.

Some control of emotion can be achieved by controlling its outward manifestations. An individual who maintains an appearance of calmness has taken the first step toward being really calm. The various features of an emotional reaction tend to reinforce each other. Lack of control makes the visceral responses more intense and therefore makes the total emotion greater. Control of one's actions, manner and speech help to inhibit the visceral response. Probably more harm has been done by uncontrolled emotional reactions than by any reasonable attempt to control them. However, some activity in response to an emotion is to help as an outlet to the pent-up feelings and urges caused by emotion, for that was Nature's intent in providing the nerve and gland responses as a means of survival for the individual.

For example, if a person in grief can, preferably alone "cry it out" there will probably be a release of tension that will enable that person to better stand up under the remainder of the period of grief. However, such release can not be allowed to grow so that it is all-consuming in energy and gets entirely out of control. A reasonable release of such tension will prove beneficial.

A situation becomes less fearful when its nature is investigated intelligently. Intellectual response to situations perhaps represents the cortical inhibitions of crude thalmic activity, and thus controls emotion in a way that can be understood physiologically. The reason that more people do not have emotional control is probably because they do not want it. A person who secures his ends by angry blustering or who gains sympathy by being fearful will not readily overcome these habits. The control of emotion will not be obtained by mere wishing, but can be achieved through the use of principles basic to all habit formation, such as motivation, practice and success.

Lasting states of emotions after the original stimulus has ceased to exist accounts for the conditions of persistence, ambition, rivalry, cooperation, stubbornness, moodiness, fearfulness. These qualities all have social value in their motivating drives. Emotional development is thus especially important in the formation of traits of personality. It is habit forming and lasting.

CHAPTER VI

ADJUSTMENTS TO MENTAL CONFLICT

Causes of Tension

The greatest problem of practical psychology is that of adjustment. Adjustment may be defined as a matter of finding comfort or satisfaction. A person may be said to be in a state of non-adjustment when he is uneasy or discontented; he is in a state of adjustment when he is enjoying relaxation and peace of mind. He is in a state of non-adjustment when he suffers from unsatisfied cravings or desires; he has made his adjustment when these cravings or desires have ceased to trouble him.

It is always in conditions of dissatisfaction or non-adjustment that neuroses develop. No man ever developed a neurosis in any situation in which he was satisfied and at ease. Neurotic-producing conditions are those that arouse impulses and desires from which the individual is unable to find relief.

Craving or unsatisfied desire is the manifestation of an underlying state of nervous tension; satisfaction is the feeling which is experienced when this tension is relieved. Life is a never-ending series of reactions to the demands that are made upon all persons by the situations of life.

The life of the individual is a constant struggle to achieve satisfaction and escape dissatisfaction, to get pleasure and avoid pain. But satisfaction and dissatisfaction, pleasure and pain, and the entire gamut of emotions are merely manifestations of underlying processes rooted partly in inherited tendencies and partly in acquired inclinations. Expressed in physiological terms, the struggle for satisfaction really amounts to a continual effort to find relief from the states of nervous tension produced by the various stimuli to which the organism is subjected. It is, in other words, a struggle for adjustment.

Pleasure versus Pain

"What causes people to do the things they do?" is a question everyone has asked at some time or other. At times we have wondered at the actions of some other person, perhaps have wondered at our own actions.

All living matter is composed of protoplasm. This is the substance that gives life to matter. Protoplasm is very sensitive to outside stimulus; it is easily irritated. Its constant aim is toward the pleasant and away from the unpleasant; in other words, it desires pleasure and dislikes pain; it favors pleasant sensations and shuns the unpleasant. This reaction is common in all forms of living matter, it is fundamental.

Since protoplasm is the fundamental material of which all living cells are composed, man is made of this substance, and he reacts just as the smallest cell reacts. The human body is a vast accumulation of living cells, so constituted as to become a complex organism. Man, therefore, reacts just as protoplasm reacts—toward the pleasant and away from the unpleasant. The course of action that ultimately will bring the greater satisfaction —the desired comforts of life, the most pleasurable and satisfying experiences—is the course to be followed. It is to this end that human activities are directed, and naturally so.

Like the original and fundamental protoplasm, toward the pleasant and away from the unpleasant—this is why people behave as they do.

Each of the emotions which humans experience— love, liking, fear, anger, dismay, confusion, bewilderment, homesickness, loyalty, patriotism, disgust, resentment, antagonism, joy, despair, aspiration, grief, jealousy, happiness, sorrow—is a variation of the two basic emotional effects—pleasure and pain. The desire of every person is to escape pain and find pleasure. Every satisfying experience becomes desirable while every unpleasant situation is to be shunned. Man has evolved a complete set of techniques, or mechanisms, by which to attain his goals. Some of these are beneficial, while some are self-defeating. If they make for health, happiness, effectiveness, then obviously they are satisfactory, and vice versa.

Psychologic Mechanisms or
Substitute Adjustments

Psychologic mechanisms or substitute adjustments are devices by which man attempts to meet his problems, to satisfy his wishes, his desires, and to escape dangers and painful experiences. These fall into two categories: (1) defense mechanisms and (2) pleasure substitute mechanisms. The pleasure-pain motive underlies all actions.

Thanks to the faculties of memory and creative imagination, man has a greatly broadened scope of experience; he is able to live in the past and future as well as the present. The way in which these abilities are used determines whether they are assets or liabilities. Psychologic mechanisms are probably not recognized by the person using them, because he or she is so habituated to them as to be entirely unaware of them.

Funeral directors must serve people with different personalities and varied mental and emotional reactions. Therefore, it is useful to present the fundamental psychological principles underlying these differences.

Everyone, however insignificant he may seem to others, is tremendously important to himself. Observe conversation, your own as well as that of others, and notice how often the personal pronoun "I" and the possessive pronoun "my" appear. We are inclined to interpret everything in terms of how it affects our own welfare. We want food when we are hungry. We wish for fame and recognition from our fellow humans. We seek physical protection. We desire respect for our opinions. There are countless ways in which we build up, fortify, satisfy, and aggrandize our ego. Since nobody else feels the same tender solicitude for my own ego that I do, it is inevitable that I am to have ego-wounding experiences. There are multitudinous ways in which this "ego" can be endangered or hurt.

The individual who does things that later hurt his conscience has injured his own ego and his own self respect. Other persons, thinking primarily of their own desires, are going to injure his feelings of importance. These experiences are constant throughout life.

Heredity and environment are determined for us. I am a part of all my ancestors, people whom for the most part I do not know. I did not choose my heredity, nor can I change it. I can have nothing to say of the environment into which I was born. I can change it to a limited degree, but my control over this environment is very limited. I can do little about it, except perhaps to leave it.

(1) Defense Mechanisms

It is not only my experiences that are important, but also the way in which I react to them. It is not what happens to me that is so important, but it is how I take it. We have, then, three factors: heredity, environment, and personal response. The first two are given to each individual; the third is the individual's sole responsibility.

Repression

Many experiences must be forgotten. However, forgetting is not an easy or simple thing to do. This brings in the factor of **repression**. True forgetting would mean to eliminate all emotion, and that is practically impossible. A girl going to her first dance may slip and fall in the middle of the dance floor. She can never forget such an embarrassing experience. At the time she will feel socially ruined, because her pride was hurt. A young man's best girl jilts him for the champion football player of the school. This is a wound that he cannot, in the case of most young men at least, treat lightly. He has "lost face." While in both of these instances the individuals will get over their painful experiences without any noticeable permanent injury, nevertheless such experiences cannot help but make some change in the individual's personality, in his attitude toward similar possibilities in the future, and in his future feelings. He will repress such memories, probably, although not able to forget them entirely.

Two things happen when memories are repressed. Because their associated emotional tone is still operative, these memories continue to live and are constantly being evoked whenever any stimulus of similar nature causes them to be recalled the very thought of such memories is embarrassing or irritating. The experience has not been forgotten, but the emotion of it has been dammed up, repressed. The second thing that may happen is that the emotion which has been repressed may give rise to other psychologic mechanisms, as a "complex." Such complex may have an intimidating effect on the individual, causing her never to want to attend another dance, or causing him to avoid all feminine company in the future. If the emotion of the experience is repressed, the lack of a proper outlet may change the individual's personality, attitude toward life, toward other people, or toward himself, causing lack of self-confidence.

Whether repression will cause such drastic changes will be determined by the severity of the wound and the type of personality involved. Everyone represses memories of painful experiences without serious results, but frequently these experiences cause maladjustments.

To face painful experiences is not easy, far from it. It is, however, less difficult in the long run than experiencing the complications bred by repression. Just the same as applying medicine to an injury: it hurts severely for a time, but is much better than the infection that will result if the medicines were not applied.

Withdrawal

Withdrawal is the adjustment that comes from the desire to avoid hurting one's ego. Temporary withdrawal may be the best course of procedure. A person may withdraw from associations that are harmful or profitless. Every human being needs places and times of rest and quiet, temporary escapes from the noise, confusion or worry of the day. Such withdrawal is desirable and necessary, provided it is not exercised too much.

When withdrawal is used as a permanent escape and when it is grounded in fear, it becomes detrimental. The hermit is a person who has adopted permanent withdrawal. The returned crippled veteran might find it desirable to withdraw from soicety to avoid any semblance of pity, to avoid "being in the way" of others. Psychologic withdrawal that is permanent or that is founded on fear—fear of being hurt, fear of being disregarded, fear of reality—is dangerous to the individual's personality.

Too many people withdraw from reading or listening to anything that is disturbing to their opinions; they will not listen to anyone who disagrees with them. They will not consider another side of a problem. No person or group of persons has any monopoly on the proper solution to any question, so should not withdraw from facing a problem by withdrawing from outside influence, by literally building a "wall of China" around their cherished opinions.

Regression

Regression is a reversion to an infantile level of behavior and occurs when a person is faced with disappointment, annoyance or frustration. He "acts like a spoiled child." The spoiled child has two favorite techniques by which to control his environment and assure gratification of his desires: temper tantrums and sulking. If the child, or the adult, can gain his ends by such behavior it will become a permanent mode of action. Such behavior is bad enough in small children but is inexcusable in adults.

Fixation

Fixation is a psychologic mechanism wherein a person rivets his attention and focuses his emotional force on some one idea or action, or at a given level of adjustment. There are individuals who have a mother fixation and find it impossible to find happiness away from "mother." Racial fixation finds the individual unable to see any good qualities in any race but his own and further feels that his race is due all the honor, homage and adulation, or, conversely, that a hated race is a scourge and should be destroyed. Another man may consider wealth or social prestige or some other quality as his criterion.

The harm of the psychologic mechanism of fixation, lies in its excessiveness. To love one's neighborhood, one's mother, one's country, one's race, one's position among his fellow men, is natural and desirable. It is only when such attitudes become exclusive, when they lead to suspicion, distrust and hatred of all outside this sphere that they become destructive and eventually self-defeating.

Man's ability to adjust to environment demands, to adapt himself to changing conditions and necessities, is one of the major elements in his survival. The trouble with fixations is that they reflect rigidity and inflexibility which are bound to be self-defeating, since change is forever characteristic of life itself. Customs and modes of life change from generation to generation and within each lifetime. Individuals, too, must change. One cannot become fixed on an infantile level of behavior, for he then misses the rewards of maturity. We live in an ever-expanding universe. Beauty, goodness, and truth are all relative and not absolute terms. To be happy in such a world we must be capable of growing, not only physically but mentally and emotionally as well.

Dissociation

Dissociation is the denial by an individual of the existence of those attitudes, qualities or actions possessed by him but of which he does not approve. A person will severely criticize some fault in another which is characteristic of the critic. One person may be "sensitive," but the same characteristic in another is "self-pity." A chronic fault-finder criticizes another for "always finding fault" with people. A "thrifty" individual criticizes another as being a "tight-wad." Faults are easily observed in others, but unrecognized or unacknowledged, for the most part, in one's self.

Projection

Projection consists in imputing one's faults to others. Crusaders against vice fall into this category, for by continually thinking and talking about the "sins" of their fellow citizens they are projecting their own desires into others, and, in this way repressing the thought of having the weakness. To cite a specific example, a man who was blatant about his own piety and vehement against the sins of his community, led attempts to stop Sunday movies, denounced bathing beaches, opposed community dances, denounced co-educational institutions, tried to reform his community by prescribing its social life and the clothing styles of its people, finally had to leave town because of his attentions to another man's wife.

Persons suffering from persecution mania are usually projecting their self-accusations in such a way as to believe others are attempting to bring about their downfall. Further, a sense of guilt may be strong enough to cause a person to be very profuse in his statements of his own innocence in doing certain wrongs and be sure that others are accusing him. In such persons, if the facts are not faced and overcome, then fear, the most prolific of all troublemakers, continues its destructive work. Much of the time, the first person to make an accusation against another is himself the worst offender, or would be if he had the opportunity. His accusations against another are made to assure his own innocence.

Negativism

Negativism is a phase through which most children pass and may be expressed by refusing to do what is requested or by insisting on doing the opposite of what has been asked. Such attitudes are seen in adults who continually refuse to agree or cooperate with others, and may go to the extreme of actually foregoing something really desired or doing something really distasteful rather than give in. Probably no one is entirely free from this negativistic attitude, for there are persons whose manner of speaking, dogmatism or cocksureness is so irritating that they evoke antagonism from others.

Some persons who assume a negativistic attitude do so in order to give themselves a sense of superiority and courage in defending their own insecure ego. At the opposite extreme of this negativistic attitude is spineless acquiescence, and both are expressions of immaturity and insecurity, and both are ineffectual and self-defeating.

Displacement

Displacement is another protective mechanism and is used primarily to release emotional tension built up by repressed memories or immediately irritating circumstances. A man, realizing he is failing in business, blames the political party in power, his unethical competitor, or an unappreciating community, anything but himself. A woman, having experienced a bad afternoon at bridge, comes home and takes her pent-up emotional tension out on the children by punishing them for trivials that ordinarily would pass unnoticed. A man cannot tell his boss what he thinks of him, takes his temper out on his wife by complaining about the meal she has prepared, the condition of the house, the behavior of the children, or whatever attracts his attention. Tension created by suppressed emotion must be released. The proper channel for such release is some hobby, participation in sprots or civic enterprises. Some avocation requiring enthusiasm and energy offers release of pent-up emotion. Such activities are much better than merely displacing a hate to some other focus.

Irritation

Irritation is an extreme mechanism wherein an individual has allowed his irritations to become so intense as to affect all of his relationships, all of his contacts. As a drop of ink in a pail of clear water clouds the entire pail of water, such a person allows his irritations to cloud his whole life. He is a continual and constant grouch. The whole world is wrong. He may try to excuse himself in terms of his multitudinous troubles and worries, but the fact is that he has allowed his daily irritations to accumulate in his emotional system, providing no outlet for them, that he must vent a most disagreeable personality upon everyone he meets. Such a state of mind will upset his system to such an extent as to cause ill health. Like the steam in a boiler, it must have an outlet or it will build up pressure until it explodes, so an individual's emotions must have some adequate outlet as they accumulate. This is necessary for physical and mental health and for a successful social and business life. It is essential for general well-being.

The psychologic mechanisms so far considered are all **defense** mechanisms, desgined solely to protect the individual's ego from injury. There are other mechanisms, somewhat similar in nature and purpose, for the purpose of flattering or supporting the ego or providing vicarious pleasure. These are known as **pleasure-substitute** mechanisms.

(2) Pleasure-Substitute Mechanisms

All of these mechanisms tend to fail for the same reason. Our fears and our desires demand direct answers, definite solution, specific satisfaction. A false front will not satisfy the fundamental needs of the individual. A nervous driver may find looking at the slippery road too upsetting to his nerves, but disaster awaits him if he looks, instead, at the beautiful scenery at the side of the road. Most psychologic mechanisms imply basic immaturity because they denote the inability or unwillingness to face the facts, and then to attempt to overcome or change the situation.

Rationalization

Rationalization, a defense mechanism, is a process of self-justification. It is called into play whenever any cherished belief, opinion or action is challenged. A person who becomes irritated on reading or hearing an opinion expressed that is contrary to his own, has here a danger warning that he is not really thinking but is merely on the defensive. It is not the idea to which he is giving such loyalty, but his own self-esteem. The idea has value mainly because it is **his** idea, **his** opinion; therefore it is right, it should not be questioned. His decisions are absolutely right; persons differing with him are entirely wrong.

An individual who uses rationalization as a defense mechanism will usually not acknowledge making a mistake himself. To do so would wound his pride or injure his ego. Instead, he justifies his every action by excusing himself. Stinginess is rationalized by the claim that the needy would only squander and waste anything given them, that they had the same chance at becoming financially successful as anyone else. Extravagance is rationalized by the excuse that it is his money to spend as he chooses, and besides, he is keeping it in circulation. A man may rationalize his own acquisitiveness as enterprise, his stubbornness as firmness, his disregard of others' feelings as frankness, but the same quality in another as rudeness. If he fails he "never had a chance" or "would not stoop to the methods" of his successful competitors.

Compensation

A substitute adjustment, one of the most used and commonly recognized of all mechanisms, is **compensation**. This is a matter of "making up" for some lack in an individual's personality, the development of over-aggressive behavior in response to social frustration. Compensation is an overemphasis of a characteristic that serves to relieve or conceal the inability of the individual to achieve a standard set by social expectation.

Compensation in itself, if practiced wisely, is good. It can bring happiness to an individual and to those who come in contact with him that could not otherwise be possible. It can build a useful life that would otherwise be barren, unhappy or even miserable. In a way, we all compensate for our own limitations. The wise person compensates for his deficiencies by building up his assets. Much of the world's creative genius would have been lost had it not been uncovered and discovered by compensative acts. One who is very unattractive in appearance deliberately cultivated the art of conversation. A man crippled by infantile paralysis and not able to participate in sports became a successful chess player. Another, denied a college education, compensated by becoming financially independent.

Some people, however, too painfully aware of handicaps, are prone to go too far, or to act unwisely. Overcompensation results in disproportion and distortion in the development of compensatory attempts. Bullying, for example, is the result of an inferiority complex. Gossiping may be the result of a drab life. A reformer's work is often done to make up for past errors of his own.

All people compensate to some extent and usually benefit. Often a parent's pride in a child's achievements is magnified because of the parent's inability to accomplish the same result earlier in life, a desire now fulfilled in the child. A childless woman's activity in welfare work among children may be accentuated because her desire for children of her own had never been realized. A cripple's intense interest in music or literature may be the result of not being able to participate normally in childhood play or physical activities.

Compensation, if it is objectively facing one's limitations and special assets, is a psychologic mechanism of great value; if used as an escape technique it will prove harmful.

Sublimation

Sublimation is a substitute adjustment that is generally considered wholesome. Sublimation concerns itself with the direction of energy which unrealeased would produce tension symptoms. Countless frustrations, necessity of performing disagreeable tasks and postponing satisfactions, are all energy-producing. Such energy, like the steam in a boiler, must be released. To direct its release in some productive channel is the proper solution. Every worry, every anger, every irritation, every disappointment resulting in an increase in energy which if unexpended and unexpressed, results in overstimulation of the hypothalamus manifesting itself in tension symptoms.

If the highway an autoist planned to take is temporarily closed, he chooses another route or he takes the detour. If strawberry shortcake has been planned for dessert and it is discovered there are no strawberries on the market, plans are changed for some other delicious dessert instead of saying, "We won't have any dessert." A couple who lost their only son while he was in college did not grieve their lives away, but assisted needy young men through college. This couple redirected their energies in a way that accomplished good.

No individual can live a life that goes serenely on without mishaps and disappointments, without sorrows and frustrations. No person escapes trouble. No man has everything as he wishes all of the time. Under such circumstances the individual has one of two choices. He can refuse to face the issue, repress, dissociate, project, or he can sublimate in such a way that his energies are redirected in useful channels and become a source of productivity. Sublimation, then, is the result of man's ability to rechannel his energies and to use constructively and in new ways that excessive energy which unreleased would be harmful.

Phantasy Formation—Extreme Day-Dreaming

Phantasy formation is day-dreaming which has become an end rather than an incentive. Day-dreaming can be of value and assistance to spur effort toward achievement. The doer without the dream is a mere robot; the dreamer who does not at least attempt to actualize his dreams is an escapist. Dreaming is a necessary forerunner to achievement, but the dreamer must do something besides dream; he must get busy and work to achieve the thing he has dreamed.

Identification

Hero worship includes **identification**. All children have their heroes; most adults have someone whom they admire very much. Whether hero worship is desirable or undesirable depends largely on the basic worth of the hero selected for imitation and identification, and whether personality is lost or fulfilled in such identification.

It is easier to identify one's self with a person, a leader, than it is to be devoted merely to a cause. It is easier to be able to seize upon some concrete object than an abstract ideal. The world's great religions endured not only because they were based upon enduring principles and values, but also because of the personalities of their founders and leaders.

The dangers inherent in the process of identification are, of course, that the person taken as the hero may not be desirable; his errors and faults will likely be imitated, as well as his good qualities.

Conversion

Conversion is a psychologic mechanism wherein repressed thoughts are expressed indirectly in the form of symbols; and those symbols appear as disturbances of bodily functions. Conversion to a different set of ideals may change a person's entire life, either for better or worse. A person experiencing extremely revolting conditions may become so emotionally upset that he will become very ill.

Conclusion

Psychologic mechanisms or substitute adjustments are both desirable and undesirable, depending on the extent to which they are used. In his professional service the funeral director must understand the psychological reactions of many different personalities and he must realize something of the adjustments which these people may be trying to make at a time of great emotional upset. Whether an individual's attempted adjustment be that of withdrawal, repression, regression, fixation, dissociation, projection, negativism, displacement, irritation, rationalization, compensation, sublimation, conversion identification or phantasy formation, the funeral director should have an understanding of the individual's behavior. If the funeral director makes any claim to professional standing he must know these conditions. Man reacts as a total organism; when he is disturbed his total organism is involved, and the tension built up by emotional experience must find release.

If the substitute activity involves the performance of acts closely similar to those of the original activity, success in the substitute activity will reinforce the tendency to perform the original activity in the presence of appropriate cues. To the extent, on the other hand, that success in the substitute activity produces reduction of the drives which would motivate a resumption of the original activity, success in the substitute activity will reduce the likelihood of resumption of the original activity.

Substitute activity should be viewed as potentially not only drive-reducing but also simultaneously as confidence-building or confidence-reducing, depending upon the pleasure-pain results of the substitute adjustment or activity as compared with the original emotion-response reaction.

CHAPTER VII

GRIEF

Grief An Intense Emotion

The reason for the study of psychology by the funeral director, particularly for the study of emotions, is to obtain a better understanding of persons experiencing grief. As a professional man whom they have called to help them, he must understand their physical and mental condition in order that he might better serve them in their hour of need. For most people the strong emotion of grief is probably experienced fewer times in their lives than is any other emotion. But when it is experienced the need for intelligent assistance and guidance is greater than it is for any other emotional experience.

Grief is a strong emotion and is a crisis in the life of the person experiencing it. In contrast to the strong emotions of anger, fear and joy, where the physical body must be prepared for violent exertion and immediate action, the emotions of despair, grief, remorse, being of the pressing or conserving type, their nature renders such action impossible. Whereas the former emotions, demanding instant action, cause an increase in the rate and strength of heartbeat, increased rate of respiration, and a greater readiness for physical action, in contrast to this, despair and grief result in depressed pulse rate and blood pressure and in slow, superficial, and irregular breathing. Digestive processes slow or cease, causing loss of appetite or light appetite. Motivation has been reduced, probably due to the feeling of hopelessness and frustration in the situation causing the grief. Experiments have shown available strength to be at a minimum, due at least partly to the body condition as described. General observation leads to the opinion that the appetite is light and the temperature of the skin is usually lower. There is a conservative or depressing change in body economy, reducing all activity to a minimum.

Once the crisis of a strong emotion is past, the body will readjust itself in a normal way, unless the emotion continues over too long a period or is too intense for the body to be able to establish a readjustment, in which serious and permanent illness, mental or physical or both, may develop. Temperament and past experience of the individual will determine the outcome of such situations.

There have been instances of physical and mental breakdown where the emotions experienced proved to be too much for the individuals. There are cases of physical and mental pathology caused by emotions of overpowering strength or of unsupportable duration. They are seen in soldiers, physicians, and persons made ill by scenes of carnage and disaster. They are found among the patients of psychiatrists and the occupants of psychopathic wards. In such cases, under a maximum intensity or undue prolongation of emotion a more or less complete disorganization of physical and mental functions may occur. One may find loss of coordination, uncontrollable tembling, loss of control of the muscles regulating the emptying of the bladder and colon, or complete paralysis. Serious glandular disorders may ensue; or the disorganization may be largely mental involving more or less complete loss of touch with reality. Hallucinations, hysteria, and psychoses of all degrees of severity sometimes develop out of these disorganizing emotions. In general, the picture is one of thoroughgoing breakdown of normal function with hospitalization immediately necessary.

These are extreme cases, however, as such experiences occur only in a small percentage of people because most emotional experiences are of comparatively short duration and are not so intense, because the body is able to return to normal conditions when the emotional experience has passed and other interests occupy the attention of the individual.

Passive sorrow, grief, or despair seem to arise from frustrations experienced under conditions which force the individual to feel that he is completely powerless in the face of circumstances. Such emotions occur upon the death or other loss of a person who is dearly loved or upon whom one has been very dependent.

Bodily reactions to emotional stimuli are not willed movements, although the will does usually enter into the situation to the extent of modifying the individual's responses. We have seen how the average person's emotional responses are not as violent as they were many generations ago. Not that the loss felt is any less than it was in the past, not that the grief is any the less keen, but better mental control on the part of the grief-stricken is in evidence.

Early man, of course, developed systems of incantations and ceremonies of appeal to higher powers or spirits so his sufferings might be less severe. In his helpless feeling of grief caused by death of a member of his family these ceremonies, involving much physical activity and weird wailing, served a successful outlet for his strong emotions within, and ameliorated his fear of the evil spirits or divine vengeance of his gods. It is thus easy to see why and how these seemingly weird practices started. They served a purpose, both physically and psychologically.

These customs have survived, although considerably modified, in our present day religious funeral services. We still appeal to higher powers for assistance in our troubles, and some present day forms used are not so much different from those of primitive mankind. Our present day religious songs are the survival of primitive weird chants and wails. We still array our dead in his or her best clothing, a custom survival of the finery with which early man clothed his dead. We can see that human nature has not changed. We may place different interpretations on our reasons for our acts, but the fundamental principle remains the same. Such customs change very, very slowly.

Man's added knowledge of conditions has enabled him to exercise better control over his emotional expressions. Social custom changes slowly, but is less severe and exacting, more comforting, than it was even a generation ago. No longer do people emphasize their emotional expressions. It has not been many years ago that all persons "in mourning" were required to wear black clothing, not so long ago that the clergy did not consider a funeral sermon successful until all women were shrieking their grief and some of them swooning and fainting, that the bodies must remain in the home from the time of death until the funeral service, thus making the ordeal as difficult as possible for the family who must remain in the house during that time. With the dead body today removed to a modern mortuary as soon as death occurs, giving the family opportunity to regain their composure; with the minister of today bringing a brief message of comfort to the griefstricken;

with the mortician relieving the family of burdensome responsibilities and details as much as possible, the period of grief, while not felt any the less severely, is made easier. Careful attention is given to the grief-stricken by the mortician as is given to the physically ill by the physician.

Grief Denotes Helplessness

Grief probably upsets the individual more than most of the other emotions, for it is a feeling of utter helplessness. Nothing can be done to restore the former relationships. It is aroused by interference that amounts to frustration and is caused by an event that over-powers. It is the emotion of weakness, for at such times there is one principal impulse, the cry for help or assistance. The lachrymal glands, being stimulated by this emotion, produce tears and thus we have weeping in times of sorrow. There are vocalizations which can be heard as sobbing or crying. There are other bodily changes. The "lump in the throat" is a contraction of smooth muscles in the alimentary canal at the level of the throat. The skeletal muscles are weak and flabby. The bodily posture is altered. The step may falter.

Grief is a complex emotional state. The individual, being frustrated by the loss, realizes at least these two factors: (1) an appreciation of the value of that which is lost and (2) an awareness of the loss itself. It is an acute manifestation of a conflict state. The situation is not merely the physical environment, but includes the total behavioral relationships. Subjectively considered, the psychological situation includes memories, thoughts, and imaginations, as well as perceived events and objects.

The tears of grief represent a somewhat mixed emotional state, rather than pure dejection, as exemplified when a depressing situation gains a redeeming feature or when the tension of an unpleasant situation is somewhat relieved. For example, a person first stunned by the shock of a death in the family is depressed, but when an act of kindness is shown by someone or when a touching incident of the deceased person's life is recalled, then the tears come. It is an acute manifestation of a conflict state.

Other Emotions Involved

Grief, being a complex emotional state, involves many other emotions in its manifestations. There might be the emotions of guilt, envy, remorse, anger, humiliation, frustration.

There is no doubt but that many instances of grief are rendered almost impossible to check because of feelings of guilt. The griefstricken person may remember instances in which he or she was unkind to the person now deceased. Now that it is impossible to undo these unkind deeds there is the guilt complex that blocks any successful recovery of the grief situation. "If only I had not done or said this." "If only I had done more for him (or her)." "If I could only relive the past and be more kind and helpful."

Anger may enter into the situation: anger toward a doctor or nurse or business associate for things, real or imagined, that said person might have done or not done to save the one now deceased from death. While there is no self-punishment in this instance, yet the grief emotion is much harder to clear up because of the intense feeling of anger toward someone else. "That person is responsible for the death" continually remains in the thoughts of the griefstricken individual.

Feelings of enviousness toward another who has not lost a loved one by death sometimes causes more serious consequences for the griefstricken, making recovery much more difficult.

Many other emotions can and do often enter the feelings of the griefstricken, causing recovery to be much more difficult and prolonged.

Grief might be said to be an emotion of frustration because of the helplessness of the situation. Oftentimes this creates in the individual an attitude of hostility toward the world and everyone in it. The individual is unpleasant toward everyone or toward those who are closest in relationship. "Feeling sorry for one's self" accompanies these feelings in many instances. Perhaps the individual derives satisfaction in being dramatic about it all.

Prompt Adjustment Necessary

Normally a state of grief remains until the individual can make some readjustment to changed circumstances. The acquiring of new interests or moving to other surroundings or merely keeping busy will aid in the readjustment. Nonadjustment to this as well as to all other emotional reactions results in nervousness and worry. If an individual remains in a stirred up emotional state for a considerable period he lacks nutritional energy to maintain normal bodily processes at a normal level. Such a condition causes improper digestion, resulting in loss of weight; he literally "worries himself thin." Such organic disabilities arise from purely psychological causes, mainly from persistent nonadjustment to baffling difficulties. Many so-called "nervous breakdowns" are severe, persistent, non-adjustive emotional reactions.

The greatest failures of adjustment are found in the lives of persons who become mentally disordered and cannot get along in ordinary social environment. Most mentally deranged persons are individuals who are bewildered by the world and can not adjust to it.

This emphasizes the necessity of griefstricken persons acquiring new interests as an aid in readjustment. This is seemingly easy for some persons but extremely difficult for others. From more or less superficial observation it appears that those who display the greatest emotional outbursts for a short time after the death of a loved one are the ones who recover more quickly, while those who maintain a calmer mien are really the ones suffering from severe shock, and take the longest time to recover. In fact, some may never completely regain emotional stability. Emotional outbursts in times of grief furnish the only outlet at the time for the pent-up feelings within. After the first shock is over the individual may find an outlet in outside activities that requires total thought and attention and considerable energy.

The first mental reaction to the loss by death is, of course, that of shock. The persons suffering the loss are at first stunned. This is especially true if the death is sudden and unexpected, but it is also a typical reaction if death results from illness, for there is almost always held out a hope for recovery. As a result of shock, few persons are able to think clearly for a time. Since every emotion must find some bodily expression, so those experiencing grief, or at first shock, will express some physical mannerism. Some will weep, some will find mixed expressions, some will faint. One person will tremble, another will choke up so that he cannot speak, another will speak in a hoarse voice, or will want to be alone. When tension is present there is always some physical expression, such as chewing a cigar, drumming on a table, tearing up a piece of paper. These expressions show that the individual feels himself too much confronted by some situation.

The term "frozen grief" has been applied to the most dramatic of the abnormal bereavement reaction— the kind that is repressed or blocked instead of finding natural expression. The victim of frozen grief wears a mask of resignation, indifference or even cheerfulness while the choked-up grief seethes inwardly. Blocked from normal emotional outlet, it sometimes erupts within the body, finding indirect expression in a physical disease. The intestinal tract, which seems to be the weakest link in the body's defenses against emotional assaults, is hit hardest and most often. Frozen grief, in a surprisingly large number of cases, actually seems to tear at the lining of the colon, resulting in ulcerative colitis. Not that the grief alone causes ulcers of the colon, but such grief in addition to an already nervous or upset condition in an individual often proves to be the precipitation of the onset of such disease.

A survey in one large hospital revealed that three out of every four cases of ulcers of the colon were definitely associated with grief situations. Such physical symptoms sometimes appear in a short time, sometimes it takes years.

Just why the intestinal tract should be especially vulnerable to the inroads of emotional tension is not completely understood. One of the medical problems of the last war was the widespread incidence of peptic ulcers among military personnel. Many of these cases were traced directly to chronic anxieties, repressed fears and other morbid states of emotional tension.

Most people, of course, get over their grief reactions normally and manage to adjust themselves to the loss of loved ones. They are able to release themselves from the ties that bound them to the deceased.

William Shakespeare gave good psychological advice when he wrote:

"Give sorrow words; the grief that does not speak Whispers the o'er-fraught heart and bids it break."

Shock treatments are often given patients who cannot seem to return to normal after experiencing extreme emotional upsets, and usually with satisfactory results.

Under our normal living conditions it is an alarming condition when every year nervous and mental disease takes a larger toll than cancer, infantile paralysis and tuberculosis combined. Some medical authorities say that one of every twenty-two Americans is doomed to spend part of his life in a mental hospital.

Satisfactory Outlets Difficult

Satisfactory outlets for the strong emotion of grief are few. Weeping is the only physical outlet provided by nature, for grief denotes helplessness and the emotional state in weeping is the feeling of helplessness. The cry of anger is the cry of helpless anger; anger that is not helpless expresses itself in some other way than crying; and the same is true of hunger, pain and discomfort. Crying, or weeping, is the reaction appropriate to a condition where the individual cannot help himself, where he wants something but is powerless to get it. A person who can "have a good cry" when in grief usually feels better for it. Yielding to the impulse to give up in the face of insurmountable obstacles often brings relief, although this is not what could be termed a satisfactory physical outlet.

Arranging and providing a funeral service as a token of respect to the memory of the departed serves as an outlet for the emotion of grief caused by the death of a loved one. This is almost always arranged according to the custom of the particular community and religion. Because a funeral service is usually a religious service, it gives comfort to those who mourn the death. While this cannot be termed an outlet for the emotion, perhaps it does ease the turmoil within the individual who now feels that everything has been done that can be done, since the life cannot be restored.

One prominent woman expressed herself as follows when experiencing a death in her family: "The time that one goes through between death and final laying to rest of any human being is, for the people who are deeply concerned, a period when one feels almost suspended in space. Life must go on. The things that have to be done, must be done. The jobs and the interests which are shoved aside temporarily, must not be completely neglected, because some day very soon they must be taken up again. Yet, always in the background is the thought that out of life forever has gone someone who is a vital, active factor, and who never again will be present except in memory."

At a later time, on the death of her husband, she

wrote: "Of one thing I am sure. When people's hearts are freed by sympathy and sorrow it makes them wonderfully kind. I have had evidence of this during the past few days. My husband's friends and associates have come to assure me of their desire to help me in any way." These sentiments were written by the wife of a President of the United States, Mrs. Franklin D. Roosevelt, a woman who was capable of adjusting herself to all conditions, and one who always maintained the most active outside interests.

One lady who was on the train, having been called to the bedside of her mother who was seriously ill, said, "I'm getting so used to tragedy I'm almost numb to it. I have two sons in action in the war, and they are at the front now. A third son is expecting to go overseas any time." One's nervous system can become tired and weary, even numb, by continued shock. This was also evidenced by another lady who, on the death of her husband, said, the day following the death, "Honestly, I do not know what I'm doing part of the time. I feel numb all over."

An emotion grows in proportion to the failure to provide an adaptive reaction or a successful outlet. The person who can dismiss trouble and worry from his mind by substituting other interest is, indeed, much the better for this ability. Just so, the woman who can "have a good cry" is greatly relieved for it. Another person who inhibits this natural expression of grief finds himself feeling as "stuffy" emotionally as he would feel physically had he eaten too much food. Weeping is the natural outlet provided by nature to relieve our systems of the strong emotion of sorrow, and a person is no doubt greatly relieved by giving way to this impulse for a short time, until he "gets it out of his system."

Among primitive peoples the most common ceremonial expressions of grief are simple exaggerations of the natural expressions of emotions, (1) carelessness as to usual comforts, and (2) a positive distracting agony. Fasting, neglecting the hair, wearing rags or sackcloth, sitting in ashes, daubing oneself with mud or pigment, are almost universal examples of the one, while wringing the hands, tearing the hair, shaving the head, beating the breast, are common examples of the other. Old Testament Hebrews donned sackcloth and ashes to show grief. The native Hawaiians gashed themselves, knocked out front teeth, cut off a finger joint or an ear, and on the death of a king the nation feigned madness as a ceremonial expression of a sorrow which had driven them frantic.

In our present day social customs, while there is not the same hysteria that was evidenced by many primitive tribes, yet there are some who reach a close proximity to those ancient and primitive customs in at least some respects. There are those who enjoy a spotlight complex whenever the opportunity arises, and this period of grief gives them a splendid opportunity. It is at such times that many persons, particularly women, will scream, others will faint. While such expressions of feeling are sometimes real and can not be restrained, oftentimes they are "put on" merely to attract attention. Such desire often arises from an inferiority complex. These people feel they are not sufficiently recognized under normal conditions and here is their chance to get all the attention they wish. Many times persons, members of a bereaved family, will appear normal in every act, never giving any sign of feeling their grief, until they find themselves in the presence of other people. Of course, there is nothing to do with screaming women but to let them scream, but a strong whiff of smelling salts will usually end a spell of fainting.

Sympathetic Understanding Necessary

It should not be assumed that all such emotional outbursts are mere "show." Much hysteria in times of grief is the result of overtaut nerves or of a real feeling of grief. At any rate, it should be so considered by the funeral director serving those families. He must consider that every hysterical symptom is part of an emotional reaction and has a more or less direct relation to tension-reduction. Such symptoms are accentuated by the presence of other persons; the complaints and the distress of the patient seem to be more marked when others are at hand. This suggests that a sympathetic attitude is one of the things which is sought in all of these cases. Any hysterical manifestation is based on an emotional state, and the emotion, in turn is a reaction to the situation which is confronting the individual at the time.

Members of every grief-stricken family do need attention and service, regardless of their emotional makeup. No emotional attitude can be fully explained without knowledge of the life situation and the history of the person who exhibits it. No two persons react in exactly the same way, but regardless of their manner of showing their feelings, or whether they appear to show them at all, they do feel the shock and grief of a great loss. People are never fully prepared to lose a member of their family. The reason for the mortician's services, aside from actually disposing of the body is that the experience might be made as easy and comforting as possible for the family.

There is much that can be learned from mob psychology to the extent that one person can greatly influence those around him to do things which he desires them to do, yet the suggestions are made in such a way that they actually want to do the things he suggests. The desire to "keep up" with one's friends and neighbors, even though it means living beyond one's income, is another example of the power of suggestion. Suggestion is the most powerful social force there is, psychologically speaking.

Funeral Director's Attitude Calm and Sympathetic

Following this psychological principle the funeral director can, by calm suggestion at the appropriate time, direct the members of a grief-stricken family in making proper funeral arrangements and thus ease their troubled minds. They are less capable of reasoning than under normal conditions and are usually more susceptible to suggestion than at other times. They want to do the accepted thing, to follow the usual customs of their community or church.

The funeral director should be calm in manner, for his mannerisms greatly influence those he contacts. A calm, unhurried attitude, when talking to those who are mentally perturbed with sorrow, will do much to quiet them. An attitude is contagious, and persons feeling helpless in their grief are more susceptible than under normal conditions.

Comforting Memory Picture Essential

The psychological purpose for the services of the mortician is to provide a memory picture in the minds of the bereaved that will be as comforting as possible, for it is something they will carry with them the rest of their lives. This serves as a release of tension and will permit the grief-stricken to relax and rest, for the funeral service has been the only means of expression possible to provide as a result of death. The greater the release of tension the more satisfactory the service; in other words, the better the service given by the mortician, the clergy and others having a part, the more comforting the memory picture.

If any advice is to be given by the funeral director to any of the grief-stricken, perhaps the thought behind it should be: "Move ahead with confidence, and do not look back with regret." This attitude should probably do more than any other to help in the recovery back to normal—if there is any "normal"—and it is an attitude of maturity. True recovery can come only when the spirit reaches maturity. The final fact remains that until an individual can handle sorrow and grief wisely and well, there can be no coming to terms with life. The individual must realize that the remainder of his or her life is yet to be lived and that it must be lived just as satisfactorily as possible, that there are others involved whose lives and happiness may depend more or less on his or her proper adjustment to the present situation. A positive attitude toward life and toward all other persons is necessary. "The person who is gone would want me to face life with confidence, to be helpful to others, so that is what I am going to do."

Tell Children About Death

Often the funeral director is asked by parents if he thinks their children should be brought to the funeral service of a family member or close family friend. One answer that is always safe to give is to suggest that if the children wish to come to the service, by all means bring them. However—if they do not wish to come, then do not force them to do so. This would also apply in having a child view a dead body.

Some parents try to protect their children against the reality of death by not talking about it and, as much as possible, by keeping them from direct experience with death when it touches their lives. As a result, when death suddenly becomes unavoidable in a child's experience he is totally unprepared to meet it and, therefore, it frequently has traumatic effects, often extending into his adult years.

A recent study of children's fears revealed that 80% of their fears were concerned with death; the children worried about dying or being killed or about someone in their own family dying.

Articles and books have been written in recent years on the subject of telling children about death. "When a child inquires about death," writes one author, "we need first to ask ourselves why he is asking. Often his immediate need is not an intellectual explanation but an unexpressed need for reassurance and emotional security. Back of a child's questions about death often lies anxiety or fear—fear that those he loves and who care for him may die and he will be left alone. Our first response may need to be one of understanding and reassurance."

Parents will help their children in facing death if they can talk naturally with them about it before an emotional crisis arises. Children have an insatiable curiosity. Many casual occasions occur, such as driving past a cemetery or looking at a newspaper picture of someone who has died, when parents and children have an opportunity to talk unemotionally about death; children can ask the questions about those things that puzzle them and parents can share their thoughts and faith. Be honest in all explanations.

Parents frequently ask if a young child should attend the funeral or memorial service. Generally . . . yes. Sometimes when death occurs in a family the young child is sent away to stay with family friends and does not return until after the funeral. There is danger in this; the child senses something unusual has happened and he feels excluded.

It is wrong to tell a child that "Grandpa has gone on a long trip" because the child will expect Grandpa to return and wonder why Grandpa didn't tell him about the trip. The child is disappointed with Grandpa—and he will remember. When Grandpa does not return some explanation must be given to the child. Better to explain the truth in the first place, thus avoiding loss of confidence by the child in his parents or whomever it was who told him about Grandpa going on a trip. The child can often understand the truth better than we might think he can. If he understands that death is a part of life, a part of nature's plan, or of God's plan, that is all for the good for all of us, he will take it and understand it the same as he understands birth or illness or any other fact of life. Happenings in the world are new to him and he wants to know why these things happen. He must be told the truth. He will develop into a better adjusted individual as he grows up and matures if he knows the truth from small childhood.

Tell the child the truth about death, answer his questions truthfully, then he will maintain a normal, healthy attitude because of knowing the facts.

CHAPTER VIII

SENTIMENT

Why Funeral Services?

A thoroughly "practical" person might ask the question, "Why make all this fuss and spend all this money for something that is seen for so short a time? After a funeral service is over there is nothing tangible to show for all of this extravagant outlay. How much more good this money would do if it were given to charity or to an educational endowment or any one of a number of other needy causes! Why throw it away on a funeral?"

We might well ask ourselves, "Just why do we do these things; Why do we have funeral services? What is back of it all, anyway?"

The "practical" person would answer, probably, by saying, "If you want the real reason for such silly and unnecessary extravagance, look at the businesses that are maintained by the custom, the mortuaries, the casket manufacturers, the supply houses, the hearse companies, the monument dealers, cemeteries, crematories, mausoleums, and countless others who profit indirectly. They promote such extravagance. They are the reason for all this."

To the casual onlooker this line of reasoning might be quite convincing. He would really doubt the good judgment, the practicability, even the common sense of such apparent extravagance "just because someone died and the body has to be disposed of." He might even ask further, "Why have a funeral service at all?

It just gets the family worked up emotionally and is hard on all concerned. Funerals make people sad when they should be enjoying life. After all, everyone has to die sometime. Why make all this fuss about it?"

To some persons, sentiment is a sign of weakness. Or at least, so they reason within themselves. To show emotion denotes a weakness in character. This line of reasoning has been going on ever since the beginning of written records, and probably it was argued long before that. Ever since man's development permitted him to debate within himself and with his fellow man there have probably been certain individuals who tried to throw out emotion and sentiment by making it appear trivial, weak, of no consequence, and to discard manifestations of it as being extravagant displays and wasted substance and energy.

But throughout history no such attempts have ever been successful. Humans have always maintained some means of expressing their emotions in tangible ways. At times their customs in expressing these sentiments have seemed to reach unwarranted heights of extravagant display, pomp and ceremony. Certain rulers have impoverished their little nations to build monuments to deceased members of their royal families. Much national wealth has been squandered in such extravagant displays that apparently accomplished no practical good. We see today some of these monuments that have stood for centuries — the Egyptian pyramids. But down through history mankind has continued to give vent to his feelings in such "extravagant" display, to display his feelings of sentiment for a person or a cause, even though it has meant material sacrifice.

One thing holds true, though all else may cease to exist as such. It is this: *Human Nature Does Not Change. Customs change to some extent, but the reasons for those customs remain the same. Man's fundamental needs are the same now as they have been since there was man. His outward forms of expression may assume a difference in appearance from time to time, but the meaning behind it, the reason for it, the sentiment in it remains the same.

Human Feelings Paramount

Man's feelings, his emotions, are the controlling factors in everything that he does. Even the "practical" person in criticizing "extravagant displays" of feeling is being guided by emotion, though it may be expressed through the form of a defense mechanism, a substitute reaction, which was studied in Chapter VI.

General Dawes once said, "When men have come together around the long green conference table, and when great issues are at stake, the outcome of their discussion depends more upon the psychology that lies below the chin than upon the psychology that lies above it." In other words, men are moved less by what they think and see and hear than by how they feel toward one another and toward the situation that confronts them. Probably all of us make our choices and act upon the basis of what we like and dislike and hope and want, then later we think out reasons by which we justify ourselves.

There is fundamentally no need for the funeral director to fear any great change in the public's cus-

*There are philosophical lines of thought to the contrary, but for all practical purposes in this discourse, we still maintain, **Human nature does not change.**

tomary method of caring for the dead. Reformers may come and reformers may go, but they are not going to change human nature, they are not going to prevent man from giving expressions to his sentiments, "extravagantly" if he desires, and in giving this expression according to the accepted custom of his community and his religious belief. Emotion, or feeling, is the motivating power in all life. Such a fundamental factor is not going to be uprooted by any attempted practical reasoning or any other method. It will always remain.

That reverence for the memory of the dead is too deeply rooted in human nature to be lost has been proven more forcibly than perhaps anywhere else in the reverent manner in which our soldier dead have been buried in the many little cemeteries in all parts of the world during World War II. Men who, engaged in fighting to the death with the enemy, did not become so hardened as to lose any of the sentiment for proper care of and attention to the dead bodies of their fellows. All of the care was given those bodies that conditions would allow. One look at the neatly arranged little cemeteries in the many islands and lands over the earth will convince anyone of this fact. Burial at sea, when necessary, is always observed in a most sacred and reverent manner.

The military services have not overlooked sentiment, for always an escort was sent, at government expense, with the body of the service man, to its burial place. This is, perhaps, a little thing, but the sentiment involved is the thing that counts. No one who has not experienced such an event can realize the appreciation of the deceased man's family at having the escort sent, for he is the nearest representative, at the moment, to the one they have just lost.

Funeral Customs Develop Slowly

A Supreme Court Justice some time ago said: "No cultural activity of which we have knowledge antedates the ceremonial disposition of the dead, and there is no prospect of these practices being abandoned."

Our American burial customs were not devised by funeral directors or by anyone else. They developed over a period of a great many years, stemming from many different religions, lands and ages. They vary not a little even among Americans, due to the influence of religion, racial antecedents, local customs, individual views and other factors. They are deeply rooted and founded on tradition. They cannot be changed easily or quickly, nor can they be regimented, here in America. Even though some such customs may seem pagan or grotesque to an outsider, let him not forget that these customs afford comfort to those persons who are the most concerned directly with the funeral, the heartbroken family of the deceased. Who then, would wish to deny the bereaved mother, wife or child that comfort?

This sentiment as expressed in the reverence shown the dead is the spirit which has brought about present-day American funeral standards. It is the ideal upon which our funeral directing profession has been built and it will survive because it stems from the deep feeling, the sentiment, that lies within every individual.

Another deep-rooted desire within every normal person is the desire for improvement. He wants, when it is available, a better car, a better radio, a better home, better implements with which to work, all of which make for a better life. The quick adoption of the better methods of transporation prove man's innate desire for improvement. He may not demand it, but as soon as it is provided he will want it. The pioneers of our western country made the trip in covered wagons, for that was then the best method of travel across the new and unexplored country. Man of today would not be satisfied with such slow travel. The automobile replaced the horse, the airplane is replacing the automobile, and although we might not know what will replace the airplane, something better will evolve. Jet-propelled aircraft is outmoding planes with propellers.

The same is happening in the funeral profession. It is less than a hundred years that arterial embalming was practiced for the purpose of preservation for funeral purposes. The public did not demand embalming, but once it had been made available they readily accepted it. The public did not demand caskets in place of coffins, but once the new receptacles were offered there was no further market for the old kite-shaped burial case. The public did not demand funeral homes, but once such facilities were made available it welcomed them. The public did not demand lowering devices, but once such machines had been introduced all funeral directors had to include such device as part of their equipment. No matter what it is, if a thing has merit the American public will welcome it, want it, pay for it.

Human Emotion Must Be Satisfied

It is interesting to note that the contracts of the army and navy during World War II learned not to make price the determining factor in the choice of a mortuary,

but instructed their contract men to select the establishment best qualified to give proper service. Price was
no longer the determining factor, but a reputation for
quality service and professional ethics was made the
determining factors. These military departments had
learned that their primary obligation to their men and
to those men's families was to see that the bodies of
their deceased men were given the best care available.
The sentiment of the public demanded it.

Through the Red Cross the amy and navy cooper-
ated to the fullest extent in seeing that a soldier or a
sailor got home to attend the funeral of a member of
his family. In this way the sentiment involved was
recognized if the man in question was within the bounds
of the country so that the trip home was a possibility.

In the statement issued to prospective mortuary
bidders for veterans' funeral services there was the
following specification:

"Within the limits specified in the proposal, contract will be awarded on a **quality** basis . . . . . In making
the award, consideration will be given to the quality of
supplies and materials to be furnished; the quality of
professional services by a competent staff; adequate
funeral establishment and service facilities; necessary
rolling stock and other equipment; generally recognized
reliability in professional and business matters; and
financial responsibility.

"What the contractor must do was to perform his
work in such a manner as to insure services of the
highest type and thus of a character that can result in
no criticism to the Government."

In a special letter regarding the proposed contract there was the following paragraph:

"The Veterans' Administration realizes that it has a great responsibility in looking after the needs of the Veteran; however, it is not unmindful of the fact that it also has a great responsibility in properly caring for the remains of those who die after serving their country. Every effort will be made by the Veterans' Administration to insure the proper care of the dead to the end that in every case where the remains of a deceased veteran are buried by the Veterans' Administration, or are returned to his loved ones, that in death as in life the Government has fulfilled its duty to those who have served their country with honor."

While there are grave doubts in the minds of many morticians as to their ability to perform the services and furnish the merchandise required at the price the Government will pay for such service and merchandise, nevertheless the one redeeming factor in it all is that the Government demands good quality of both service and merchandise and from a funeral establishment that is able and willing to fulfill such contract. There is the realization of the sentiment in the feelings of the bereaved regarding the proper treatment of the body of their loved ones.

There is one thought that must remain paramount with every agency serving the public, whether it be a government agency or a business or professional man, and that is the fact that the emotional feelings, the sentiment of individuals must be recognized, must be satisfied, and all service to them must be on that basis if it is to be at all satisfactory. Since human nature does not change there will never be any loss in sentiment. In order to render satisfactory service, then, those serving must keep this thought paramount.

Sentiment Is Life Itself

What is sentiment? Why is it so deep-rooted? Sentiment can be defined as emotional attitude; it is the way a person feels toward or about something. Without sentiment there would be nothing in life that would be worth while. Everything we do, everything we have in life that is worth while depends entirely on sentiment. Our family life, our humanitarian movements, even our entire civilization itself is sentiment. Strong character results from the harmonious organization of the sentiments. To be founded upon sentiment, then, is the finest thing that can be said of our funeral profession, for sentiment consists of those finer elements in human living. It is the thing that makes happiness, that makes life worth while.

It is those little sentimental acts people do that is life itself. Bare living without sentiment would be nothing. Of what does life consist? Material things are destructible and are only a means to an end. Happiness and comfort are the things we desire, the things that make for us pleasant memories that will be with us all our lives. That is sentiment and that is good living.

Our funeral profession is founded entirely upon sentiment, as is religion, art, literature, even science, all of the finer things of life. We must do everything in our power to keep it on a high plane.

Money Buys Contentment

We frequently hear people say things regarding funeral and burial customs that they do not really mean. We have all heard people talk at quite some length on the foolishness of spending money to buy a casket, then bury it in the ground or cremate it. It is visible for only a short time and it can not do the dead any good. Yet, these same persons will show the same feeling, the same sentiment, for the care of their loved ones who die as will anyone else. When the time comes to select a casket for a member of their family they will do the customary thing, buy something appealing that is within their means. It is a rare exception to find a person who acts differently from this established procedure.

Many people say, "I believe in giving flowers to the living; they do the dead no good." That is true, but who gives flowers to the dead? Flowers that are sent to funeral services are given for the benefit of the surviving family, out of memory of the one who has died. It is only on occasions of special concern, or some special event, usually, that flowers are given to persons, such as an anniversary, at a time of illness, a funeral, and in each one of these instances sentiment is the important factor.

People spare no expense or effort to recover a drowned body. Yet, what do they do after the body is found? Following appropriate services they take it to the cemetery and bury it. The recovery of the body and its burial was to them mental comfort. How else could have money been spent that would have given those people any more satisfaction?

As is oftentimes argued, money spent for a funeral leaves nothing tangible to show after it is all over. That is true, nothing tangible is left. But is not contentment, satisfaction, comfort of more importance than money in the bank? What will money buy but pleasant memories? You take a vacation trip, and when you return what have you to show for the money the trip cost? Nothing tangible, but you do have memories of a pleasant time. You attend a concert, go to a party, attend a show, and when you return home you have nothing tangible to show for the money you spent, but you do have happy memories, memories of a pleasant evening, if you enjoyed it. At least you have memories. What else can your money buy?

Sentiment: Life's Essential Element

It is these so-called "non-essentials" that make life worth living, that are really the essentials of living. We want more than a bare existence. It is these expressions of sentiment that are really life itself. Sentiment makes life rich and of value and it is these expressions of sentiment that are worth the money they cost, whether they be in the form of providing a modern funeral service with its accompaniments, giving flowers to the bereaved family, taking a trip to some far-off place, buying nice clothes or a car, attending an opera, caring for one's family, or any one of millions of other expressions of sentiment. Without sentiment we would have nothing left.

Probably the most vital ingredient in a funeral service is the religious element. In fact, it is this element that is responsible for the funeral service, for it would be hard to visualize a funeral service without any religious thought contained in it. The funeral service originated with primitive peoples in their efforts to appease their gods and to drive away evil spirits. Modern religions today contain considerable, some more and some less, of this appeasement element, although the trend is more and more toward an attempt to comfort the bereaved survivors. There can be no closer relation than exists between funeral services and religious beliefs. This is because religion is also deeply rooted in sentiment. Religion is an individual's attitude toward what he believes is a higher power.

Commercialization a Danger

The greatest danger that exists regarding the funeral profession as we know it today is the tendency for the funeral director to become too mercenary in his attitude toward those he serves. If he thinks more strongly about the cost of a funeral service than he does of the service he can best give the bereaved family, he is too mercenary. The same is true if he advertises price above all else, and he is teaching the public to use price as their motive for calling him, rather than his service to them. Such acts take out the sentiment upon which the survival of the funeral service profession depends. True, economic survival demands attention to finances, but this must not be made the paramount feature. Sentiment must always remain the basis of all funeral services!

The one attitude the funeral director must watch most closely in himself is this: he must remember that every death call he receives is a most tragic experience for that family. It cannot be "just another case" to him, but the opportunity to serve a family in such a way that their memory of this incident will always remain in their minds as much a comfort to them as it is possible for him to make it. Even the exceptional family that appears on the surface to have no sentiment in the matter can be made to feel the sacredness of the situation by the manner in which the funeral director conducts the arrangements and counsels with them.

Sentiment Recognized

The importance of sentiment toward death and the influence of this attitude upon the nation as a whole has been expressed by the famous English statesman, Gladstone, who said, "Show me the manner in which a nation or a community cares for its dead and I will measure with mathematical exactness the tender sympathies of its people, their respect for the law of the land and their loyalty to high ideals."

Long before this time, back in the 5th century, Saint Augustine said, "The care of the funeral, the manner of burial, the pomp of obsequies are rather for the consolation of the living than of any service to the dead."

Benjamin Franklin said, "To know the character of a community, I need only to visit its cemeteries."

An official in the Office of Price Administration of the United States government during World War II said this, "Show me those who express regard for their dead and comfort their bereaved, and you show me civilization at its best" in addressing a meeting of funeral directors.

Another public official recently said, "A funeral performs the socially necessary act of interment in such a way as to be a tribute to the dead and yet also to serve the sensibilities of the survivors according to the decedent's apparent means and standing in life."

One of the best known and most widely read national business and political observers, the Kiplinger Agency, made this statement in closing one of their letters, "Emotional appeal is usually underrated by logical thoughtful persons. It's emotion, rather than logic, that sways the people at the 11th hour."

Abraham Lincoln made this statement: "Public sentiment is everything. With public sentiment nothing can fail; without it, nothing can succeed. Consequently he who moulds public opinion goes deeper than he who enacts statutes or pronounces decisions. He makes statutes or decisions possible or impossible to execute."

These statements demonstrate the importance of sentiment, especially toward death, as recognized by world leaders and moulders of public opinion.

Intrinsically a dead human body is valueless, a menace to public health. But it is not this inanimate thing which is entrusted to the funeral director. If it were, he would not be a funeral director. What is entrusted to him is the symbol of everything that body represents, everything it means, to those surviving. It is a symbol surrounded by sentiment and memories, values which are beyond price. One clergyman himself met clerical criticism of the funeral director by pointing out that "Life is enriched through symbolism and the most significant symbol of all is the human body. Casually to dismiss the body that for years has been the sign of a well-loved presence is no more admirable than lack of regard for a packet of old love letters or a worn-out Bible."

We hold funerals to bear witness of our regard and affection, to acknowledge worth and honor viture, to make recollection vivid and remembrance enduring, to enrich life with memories and to inspire it with understanding. This is the sentiment that makes life worth living, that makes it meaningful. It is life as humans live it.

Civilization Parallels Memorialization

The degree of civilization in any age of the world's past is measured by the sentiment of the people of that time in memorializing their dead. Funeral customs determine the greatness—or lack of greatness—of the people observing them. These customs determine and they reflect this greatness. Civilizations of the past have risen and fallen in direct proportion to the rise and fall in the observance of reverential care of the dead in funeral services. Historical facts of every age of mankind support this statement.

This fact is further borne out in a study of present-day cultures. Standards of living in the world today are in direct proportion to funeral observance standards. Our service men, sent to all sections of the world during the war and since, have stated that those races of mankind that give little or no thought to reverential observance of funeral and burial services maintain extremely low standards of living. The more sincere the sentiment that is shown when confronting death, the higher are the standards of living.

Those of our citizenry who criticize our American high standards in customary funeral observances should study history a little more closely, should compare recognized funeral observances in various sections of the world today, and should observe that funeral and burial customs reflect directly the stage of civilization and the standards of living and culture that these customs portray.

Psychologically, the attitude of people toward the finer and higher elements of living is reflected more clearly in their attitude toward death and memorialization than in any other way. Such attitude reveals their evaluation of the worth of man, or life itself. If the life of a human is considered cheap, so will be his final disposition; if life has value, so has the ceremony commemorating his passing.

The responsibility of funeral directors in maintaining funeral observance standards that are in keeping with desired living standards is great, indeed. If funeral directors permit burial standards to decline, then the decline of our civilization itself has already started, for such is a direct reflection. Other reasoning or arguing to the contrary, history bears out this fact in an indisputable manner, and history always repeats.

CHAPTER IX

RELIGION

Religion, the Human Common Denominator

Because a funeral service is a religious service and because the funeral director's planning leads directly to this religious service as a climax of his entire program, it seems desirable to study the significance of man's religious experience.

Every funeral director should understand the need for religious belief and observance; he should understand the release from tension provided by the religious funeral service for those in grief; he should understand religious belief as the foundation of human behavior. Briefly, he should understand the important part religious belief and practice play in human life.*

Religion is a normal product of man's conscious processes: his desires, his fears, and especially his planning for future contingencies. It is recognition by man of a controlling superhuman power entitled to obedience, reverence and worship; the feeling of the spiritual attitude of man in recognition of such a controlling power.

Observance of the most primitive existing races of men in the world today and the study of historical records dating back to the very earliest of such known records and the findings by archeologists of prehistoric specimens, all point to the conclusion that the human

---

*The subject of religion is here treated as such. No attempt is made to enumerate or to dwell on creeds, for there are several hundred creeds in the United States alone. Every religion is a spontaneous expression of a certain predominant psychological condition.

race has always been universally religious, that every group in every period of history has held to some religion, some form of ritualistic observance.

The Golden Rule

Every living religion has an object of worship, a set of rules which include both repressions and commands, moral standards, definite rewards for obedience and punishments for disobedience and almost every religion has its Golden Rule. It is interesting to note the various religious statements of the Golden Rule. Several of them, so stated, are:

Christianity: "Whatever you wish that men would do to you, do so to them."

Judaism: "Whatsoever you would that men should not do to you, do not do that to them."

Islam: "Let none of you treat a brother the way he himself would dislike to be treated."

Buddhism: "In this way should a clansman minister to his friends and familiars, by treating them as he treats himself."

Zoroastrianism: "Whatever you do not approve for yourself, do not approve for anyone else."

Taoism: "Recompense injury with kindness."

Confucianism: "What you do not want done to yourself, do not do to others."

Hinduism: "Do nothing to others which, if done to you, would cause you pain: this is the sum of duty."

Even the Greek philosophers taught a Golden Rule. Three of them, so stated are:

Socrates taught "Do not do to others what you would not wish to suffer yourself."

Aristotle taught "Treat your friends as you would want them to treat you."

Philo's dictum was "Do not do what any one is vexed to suffer."

To get a little better insight into the thinking of each of the recognized world's living religions, the following sayings from their sacred scriptures will help:

Buddhism: "Hatred is not diminished by hatred at any time. Hatred is diminished by love—this is the eternal law."—Dhammapada, 5.

Christianity: "A new commandment I give to you, that you love one another."—John 13:34.

Confucianism: Confucius was asked: "Is there one word that sums up the basis of all good conduct?" And he replied, "Is not 'reciprocity' that word? What you yourself do not desire, do not put before others."—Analects, XV.

Hinduism: "True religion is to love, as God loves them, all things, whether great or small."—Hitopadesa.

Janism: "All living beings hate pain; therefore one should not injure them or kill them. This is the essence of wisdom: not to kill anything."—Sutra-kritanga.

Judaism: "Do not do to others that which is hateful to you. This is the whole of the Law; all the rest is commentary."—Rabbi Hillil, Talmud.

Islam: "No one is a true believer until he loves for his brother what he loves for himself."—Hadith.

Shintoism: "One should not be mindful of suffering in his own life and unmindful of suffering in the lives of others."—Sacred Text of Kyo Koyen.

Taoism: "He is fit to govern who loves all people as he loves himself."—Tao-Te-King, 13.

Zoroastrianism: "On three excellent things be ever intent: good thoughts, good words, and good deeds."—Venidad XVIII, 17.

It is readily recognized, upon study, that the teachings of every religion are based on the same general principles. Every religion started on a very high plane. Every religion has deteriorated in the practices of these teachings by the followers and by the development of creeds and divisions in every one of them in later years.

Religious Development

Like all phases of human experience, religion has developed from the primitive to the present stage of culture. The problem of religious origins is connected with the problem of the nature of religion. It is helpful to understand something of the religious attitudes that have existed since the dawn of history, for it is from these religions of the past that the religions of the present have developed. In this, religion at large must not be confused with any special brand of it.

Probably the earliest religious concepts in man were the products of **fear** and the desire to protect himself from the elements. He did not understand the lightning, the thunder, the sunshine or the rain. Inasmuch as he had no control over these things, he feared them and sought a mystical or magical formula by which he could exercise some form of appeasement or regulation.

It was largely a matter of self-preservation with him. He could not control the weather, and he feared it might injure or destroy him.

Another basis for his fear appeared to him in dreams. Early man, like the small child today, could not differentiate between dreams and actual happenings. To him these experiences of his dreams had actually happened. Perhaps a deceased friend or enemy had appeared to him in a dream. From this experience he got the idea of a spirit world, of a future life after death, the idea of a dead man's ghost haunting him. He feared these things because he could not control them; he did not understand their cause. This fear led to the earliest form of worship, which was probably a form of magic. Amulets and charms were originated as forms of protection.

Animism, the belief that everything contains spirit, attributing supernatural force to material objects, was among the earliest religious beliefs. Offerings to the wind, sun-worship, and others, were the early attempts at appeasement and for gaining favor with these elements that could not be controlled.

Magic, the occult and mysterious, is in all primitive religions. The fetish, an inanimate object supposed to possess magical power, "hokus-pokus" rituals, the medicineman methods, these are all important in primitive religions. The Australian aborigines, the most primitive race in the world today, practice magic.

The next step in religious development was probably **idolatry**, this being a step higher than magic. Idols exist in many sections of the world, many times remnants of by-gone civilizations. However, many primitive tribes in existence today practice this form of religious observance.

Nature-worship, personification of nature or of phases or forces of nature, prevailed in early Greek and Roman religions. Appeasement of the dead and ancestor worship are still in evidence in some of today's religions. **Mystery** and **fear** prevail in these beliefs. The living are real and not feared; the dead are dreaded or revered.

Superstitions, such as amulets and charms and magic, not only played a most important part in early religions, but they are not entirely absent from present-day civilization. An amulet may be any object, a stone, a peice of wood, a plant, a mineral. Inscribed amulets are believed to have protective force because of the inherent power of the written word. In our own land a rabbit's foot or a lucky pocket piece is supposed to bring good luck. Will man ever progress to the point where he is entirely free from superstition?

Mature Religion

As religion progresses it gradually develops into a more nearly mature religion, conforming to the growth and development of civilization and development of civilization and of mankind in general. It is well at this point to ponder on just what is a **mature religion**. There are several points to be considered in the maturing of religious thought and belief.

1. Mature religion differs from immature or primitive religion by excluding the element of magic. In other words, as long as religion contains elements of magic it is not mature. There are many survivals of magic even in the best of man's religions today. It is to

be wondered why religion clings to certain magical practices while science generally disavows them. Some religions are freer from magic than others, and the religious experience of many individuals and groups in the great religions are, in principle at least, entirely free from magic. Some religious individuals and some religious practices, then, seem to be quite nearly mature, appear entirely free from magic.

2. Mature religion also excludes the element of literal mythology. Whatever one may think about the origin and proper uses of mythology in illustrating religious truths, certainly any insistence upon regarding myths as literally true is a mark of religious immaturity.

3. Mature religion calls for committment to truth wherever it may be found. As such, there can be no conflict between mature religion and proven scientific facts, for truth is truth and facts are facts in whatever field they may be found. In all our human relations we must be committed to the truth, if our religion is to be mature. If traditional religious cosmology is found to be in conflict with any field of knowledge, be it science, sociology or other field of research, the newly learned facts must be accepted as part of religious belief if that religion is to be mature. It is always easy to apply this test to other religious beliefs, but sometimes quite difficult to do so when our own beliefs are involved. Scientific facts cannot lessen the benefits of religious belief in man, but actually should strengthen them. Learning that the earth is not the center of the universe and is not flat does not cause present day man to be any less true to his religious principles than were the ancients. The realization that God is spirit and not a

"superman" with human passions should not in any way lessen man's religious devotion, but should strengthen it in a more nearly mature religion. We must wait until a scientific theory is well established and proven to be true before accepting it, but when it is well authenticated nothing is to be gained by dogmatic denial of such facts for the sake of some mistaken tradition. It is better to reinterpret the tradition and come out with a more nearly mature religion.

4. Mature religion reinterprets the facts of human nature. Individuals formerly believed to be "possessed of devils" or of being "bewitched" are now, in the light of psychological facts, known to be mentally ill. Many such illnesses are today capable of being cured, the same as are most physical illnesses.

5. Mature religion is ethical religion. It encourages the sensitivity of the individual to ethical relations with other individuals.

6. Mature religion interprets religious ritual and religious symbols for what they are: aids to communion with deity and in inspiring a life of love, service and purity. Prayer is another element of religious ritual needing evaluation. It cannot be used in a magical sense in a mature religion but as a means of adjusting man to universal forces and inspiring him to moral and spiritual achievement. In this way a high level of religious maturity has been achieved.

7. Mature religion is universal and all-inclusive. Early religions of mankind were tribal and nationalistic. Early gods were gods only of certain small groups or tribes. These primitive religions divided group against group, sect against sect, nation against nation and

race against race. Mature religion must possess qualities which can apply to man as man, thus unifying all of the forces of nature into one coherent unit.

8. Mature religion must possess a certain mystic sensitivity if it is to be classed as a religion, the awareness of a Presence of a Power that symbolizes the universal or the spiritual forces of life, which may be tapped for help in time of need. If freed from the characteristics of primitive religion, such an awareness should unite all characteristics of a mature religion into a vital and successful experience in life.

There is no absolute norm of a mature religion. In fact, neither religion nor science will ever reach complete and final maturity, because man will never attain perfection. To do so would render it static, at which time decadence would set in. There must always be growth and development, the striving to attain some goal beyond the distant horizon. All things, even man himself, should continually become "more nearly mature." There is no such thing as final perfection, but there should always be improvement in all things. Such must be the function of religion and of science, the gradual growth toward a better and fuller life.

The Functions of Religion

Religion gives to man what he can obtain from no other source:—a confidence in the outcome of life's struggles through a personal connection with the superior power or powers in the world. It helps him bear the troubles of life. It offers a solution of the problem of evil and improves the quality of the present life. It offers the hope of a better life in the future and outlines an ideal society for a future life. It sets a working plan of salvation.

Some kind of Deity is indispensable in religion. Personal conceptions vary greatly. Some deities are limited, some arbitrary, some just, some loving, some all-powerful.

The Supreme Being of every religion has five characteristics:

(1) It is superhuman in character and power.

(2) It is invisible even though it may be materially represented.

(3) It is controlling; i.e., it rules over human welfare and destiny.

(4) It is responsive to efforts of humans who act religiously.

(5) It is worshipful, arousing emotions of awe, reverence, trust, obedience, cooperation and submission.

Every religious human being has experience with a Deity believed to possess these five characteristics.

Almost every religion believes it has the sole duty to win the entire world to its belief.

In the emphasis placed on the various conceptions of religion, some are placed on the intellectual, some the moral, some the emotional, some on worship, some on self, some social.

In the comparison of the different religions, one or more of the following different standpoints can be taken:

(1) To condemn all religions as the outcome of superstition, bigotry, hereditary ignorance;

(2) To condemn all non-Christian religions, or all non-biblical religions;

(3) To condemn all other religions except one's own. This is a common viewpoint in most religions;

(4)   To admit good in all religions and believe each one is good for its own followers and that each is making its contribution to civilization;

(5)   To admit all religions contain some good, but are unequal, and that the world needs the best there is to be had.

The Eleven Living Religions of the World*

As a matter of interest and of helpfulness in understanding the universality of religious thought and need by mankind, there is here listed the eleven generally recognized living religions of the world today and some brief facts concerning them.

(1)   HINDUISM, founded 1500 B.C, present location India, Its deity is Brahma, its sacred scriptures the Vedas. It is known as the religion of Divine Immanence and a hereditary graded social structure. In its system are four main historic castes:

1. Brahmans, the priestly and intellectual class.

2. Kshatriyas, the rulers and warriors.

3. Vaisyas, the common agriculturists and artisans.

4. Sudras, the low-caste.

There are some 64 castes through the process of subdivision and a great many subcastes. A Hindu is in good standing as long as he has not violated the rules of caste.

Hinduism has long had attempts at reform, as far back as 557 B.C., but with little effect for the most part.

*It is not practical or desirable in this material to go into detail in explaining the world's living religions. Only a very brief statement can be made of each one. Those interested in learning more about these religions may do so through research. Every large public library has books with material on religious beliefs and practices throughout the world, from the earliest records of such down to the present.

Mahatma Ghandi tried to eliminate the caste system.

(2)   JUDAISM, founded 1200 B.C., by Moses. It is strongest in Europe and United States, but is scattered well over the world. Its deity is Jehovah, its sacred scriptures the Old Testament of the Christian Bible. It is known as the religion of obedience to the righteous God.

Judaism is the first religion to believe in one God, the world's first monotheistic religion. In the development of this thought the world owes a great debt to the ancient Hebrews. The Sacred Scriptures of Judaism represent a literary activity of about ten centuries. Zoroastrian influence during their period of captivity in Babylon was great. It was during this time that Isaiah conceived the idea of a Messiah, a political restorer.

(3)   SHINTO, founded 660 B.C., the national religion of Japan, with the Japanese emperor as its head. The deity consists of nature-gods and the emperor. It is known as the religion of nature-worship, emperor-worship and purity. Physical cleanliness is a part of the religion. Shinto teaches divine origin of the islands of Japan and that their emperor descended direct from the sun-goddess. Since World War II this nationalistic Japanese religion has become very much modified.

(4)   ZOROASTRIANISM, founded 660 B.C., by Zoroaster, located in Persia and India. Its deity is Ahura Mazda, its sacred scriptures the Avesta. Being responsible for the growth and strength of the ancient Persian empire it soon lost its missionary zeal and became stagnant. It is by far the smallest of the world's living religions today. It is the religion of struggle along with a good but limited God against the evil forces inherent in the world. Purity is the most highly prized single

virtue in Zoroastrianism. The formula occuring most frequently in the sacred scriptures is: "good thoughts, good words, good deeds." The final hope in Zoroastrianism is the ultimate triumph of moral goodness over evil spirits of the world.

(5) TAOISM. (pronounced as though the "T" were "D") founded 604 B.C., by Loa-tze, present location China. Its deity is the Tao, its scripture the Tao-Teh-King. It is known as the religion of the Divine Way.

The teachings of Taoism are: "Recompense injury with kindness." However it does not teach one to face one's difficulties, but "To withdraw into obscurity is the way to Heaven." The most characteristic single idealistic type, but it has long since degraded and lost all missionary zeal. It has always been mystical.

(6) JAINISM, founded 599 B.C., by Varhamana Mahavira, present location India. Its founder has become its deity, its scriptures the Agamas. It is quite small in number of followers, found only among the merchants of India. Jain temples of worship are among the architectural treasures of India, some of the oldest of the land. It was organized to improve Hinduism, but instead of so doing it formed a new and separate religion.

Jainism teaches transmigration of souls:—rebirth according to the previous life. Woman is condemned in its scriptures. Its importance and numbers are rapidly diminishing. Its ultimate aim is to separate entirely the soul from bodily encumbrance.

(7) BUDDHISM, founded 560 B.C., by Gautama Buddha. It is found throughout the East. Its deity soon became Buddha, its scriptures the Tripitaka. It is known as the religion of peaceful, ethical self-culture. It was the world's first religion to become international.

Buddha probably had no idea of founding a new religion. He did not teach a deity, worship or prayer. Yet he taught a moral law superior to that taught in the Hinduism from which he reacted. Nirvana, "the highest happiness," passionless peace, is Buddhist goal.

The human body is considered a miserable hindrance and life is considered as hardly worth living.

(8) CONFUCIANISM, founded 551 B.C., by Confucius. It is found in China. Its deity has become Confucius, its scriptures the Classics. It is second in size among the world's living religions. It is known as the religion of social propriety. The efforts of Confucius were entirely toward political and social reform and he remained undaunted in his work. Filial obedience and veneration, and ancestor worship, are main points of Confucianism.

(9) CHRISTIANITY, founded 30 A.D., by Jesus Christ in Palestine. It has become the most widely accepted religion in existence today. Its deity is God the Father, its scriptures the Bible. It is the world's largest in numbers of followers and has the largest number of divisions within its ranks. It is known as the religion of the love of God and love of man as revealed in Jesus Christ. It is the only religion spreading and developing mostly in the West.

The influence of its sacred scriptures, the Bible, has exceeded that of any volume written in human history many hundreds of languages. It presents most fully the saving truths of religion. Besides the 39 books of the Old Testament and the 27 books of the New Testament, contained in the Protestant Bible, the Greek and Roman Catholic churches add 14 books of the Apocrypha.

Christianity became the official religion of the Roman Empire in 325 A.D. From that date until 1054 it spread over Europe and became the official religion of all Europe, bringing about a more nearly spiritual unity in the world than there had been before or has been since, until 1517 when the Protestant Reformation became successful in much of Europe.

The conception of God in Christianity was taken from Judaism, made a God of love. The Christian teaching of forgiveness and love is unique among the religions of the world. Christianity is the only religion with a constructive personal social program for all mankind.

(10) ISLAM, founded 570 A.D., by Mohammed, present location the Moslem countries. It is one of the largest in numbers of followers. Its deity is Allah, its scriptures the Koran. The literal meaning of Islam is submission, so it is known as the religion of submission to the World-Potentate.

Mohammed united various warring Arab tribes on a new religious basis, and they have continued bound together since that time. The authority of the Koran is absolute for all Moslems. It is the most influential book in all Arabic literature. The one central thought throughout this scripture is: "There is one God, Allah, and Mohammed is his prophet." The absolute arbitrariness of Allah is repeatedly affirmed: "He guides whomsoever He pleases."

Islam accepts much of the teachings of the Old and New Testaments of the Christian Bible but regards Jesus as one of the prophets mentioned in these books, and Mohammed as the last of all prophets. It teaches conquest by force.

(11) SIKHISM, founded 1469 A.D., by Nanak, present location India. Its deity is known as the True Name, its scriptures the Granth. It is the youngest of

the world's living religions and one of the smallest. Sikhism arose as an attempt to harmonize the two most powerful religions in India: Islam and Hinduism. It is known as the religion of disciples of the One True God. Most followers today are living in their ancestral homes as peaceful agriculturists.

In Retrospect

It is interesting to note some points of similarity and dissimilarity among the world's religions.

To a certain extent all eleven religions believe in One Supreme Being, and claim of divine incarnation.

Five claim supernatural origin of the founder: viz, Buddha, Lao-tze, Mahavira, Zoroaster, Jesus.

All eleven claim divine revelation.

All have their sacred scriptures and all claim them to be divinely inspired.

Claims of miracles wrought are made by all eleven. Only Christianity, however, lays claim to its founder (Jesus) rising from the dead.

Only Christianity recognizes all mankind as sacred to God; all others regard only themselves as sacred.

The scriptures of Buddhism, Mohammedanism and Christianity command missionary work, and promote it. Jainism, Judaism and Zoroastrianism have this command in their scriptures, but they have become quiescent.

All religions teach that the spiritual life of the human individual continues beyond physical death; however, they differ widely concerning the details of future life, even concerning the desirability of a future life. All four Indian religions teach transmigration: Hinduism, Jainism, Buddhism, Sikhism. Hinduism teaches that the present life is so undesirable that it is not worth continuing. All others except Confucianism are very definite about heaven and hell.

All religions have originated in the Orient. Four originated in southern Asia, in India: Hinduism, Jainism, Buddhism and Sikhism. Three originated in eastern Asia, in China and Japan: Confucianism, Taoism and Shinto. Three originated in western Asia, in Palestine, Persia and Arabia: Zoroastrianism, Islam and Christianity. Orientals seem to have a more deeply rooted, serious religious nature than do most other peoples of the world.

Essential Principles

It is true that in the religions of ancient civilizations and in present religions of uncivilized peoples, observance of ritual is more important than adherence to faith. Ritual has played an important part in the development of religion, and religion everywhere involves a pattern of ritual, no matter how much it may emphasize faith. Among the rituals conspicuous in ancient religions were: animal sacrifice; human sacrifice in some instances; incense burning; anointing with oil and washing with water; presenting of gifts to altars; chanting of hymns and marching in processions. Every phase of life had its ritual: birth, puberty, marriage, death and burial were surrounded with religious ceremonials. Elaborate rituals were employed in preparing seed for planting, and in the eventual harvest.

The appeal to the senses is an important matter in ritual. Visual stimulation through colors and forms of vestments, stained-glass windows, flowers and movements is widespread. Organs and other musical instruments are employed, and the human voice is ritually raised in chant and song. The sense of smell is stimulated by the fumes of burning incense, and the odor of burning meat was an important stimulant in the ancient sacrifices, the assumption that it was pleasing to the gods indicating its ritual importance to men. The sense of taste was involved in the eating of sacrificed animals in the other early ceremonial meals.

Behavior influences belief. Ritualistic behavior follows a standardized or routine pattern and is the same or similar to the behavior of other persons in similar circumstances. The motivation is not essential. In fact, much of the ritual of religion is behavior that continues as habit.

The importance of ritual in religion must not be minimized. It is probable that without ritual, religion could not have developed and that religion without ritual cannot be maintained. Since man is so fundamentally gregarious, ritual becomes the social factor in religion, and faith is the personal factor. These two factors are, of course, inseparable in most religions.

Religion inherently is resistant to changes, both in itself and in all matters of personal and social life with which it is closely associated. Religion everywhere and in all times is ultraconservative; it values the antique; in any stage of its development it considers itself to have reached the ultimate phase; it lags behind the progress of culture and operates to prevent cultural advance. The notion that the antique is valuable—that the old faiths and the old ways are the best—is recognizable in almost all religions and sects. Clinging to the old as of paramount value seems to be essential for the continued life of any religion.

Changes in religion do occur, but these changes occur slowly. Perhaps this is a saving factor for civilization, acting as a balance to the exuberance of trends that might easily lead man too rapidly into unproven and unsound theories in which he might easily "lose his balance." Religious changes are the result of social changes. Social changes and scientific discoveries force new concepts in religious thinking and finally result in changes in religious belief or modification of religious ritualistic practice.

Religious Concepts

There are a great many concepts applied in the study of religion, of which several will be here mentioned in order to clarify the factors involved in its study.

Faith. Faith is an essential feature in religion. It is the belief by a person in the teachings or doctrine of the particular religion to which he belongs. He accepts such teachings as fact, regardless of their actual proof to him. This is religious faith.

Ritual. Ritual is religious behavior of a systematic sort, prescribed rites by those in authority of the particular religious organization. The significant features of ritual are: (a) The behavior is associated with religious faith; (b) The behavior is habitual, a matter of routinized action; (c) It is social: one does what others do.

Ritual has played an important part in the development of religion. Religion everywhere involves a pattern of ritual, some more than others.

Continuity. In most religions the importance of continuity and of antiquity is explicitly recognized. While it is recognized that organized religions do resist change, yet changes do occur, although such changes come slowly. Mingling of different cultures and religions necessitates change by all concerned. Social changes bring religious changes.

Custom or **Practice**. This means group accomplishment over many generations. While this could be broadened to include all forms of social life as it has been developed and passed on from generation to generation, in this particular instance it shall include only religious customs as it has grown and developed in organized religions.

Morality. Moral principles are those principles that have to do with man's relation to his fellow man. Morality is the antithesis of self-seeking. Moral actions are concerned with the promotion of the welfare of and justice toward other persons. Behavior that involves taking advantage of other persons and their welfare is 'immoral.'

Tabus or **Inhibitions.** These signify restraint of action. The system of tabus is vast and intricate in all religions. They are inseparable from social tabus, for they affect man's actions in relation to his fellow man, as well as to his object of worship.

Emotion. Emotion seems to be a feature of every religion. Certain religions and certain sects of other religions have aimed at the repression of emotion, as the Stoics. However, in most of the religions of the world the whole gamut of feelings and emotions is involved, each emotion or feeling being experienced in appropriate circumstances.

Self-Development. 'Development of character' is another phrase for this concept. Religion actually has been conceived in terms of self-seeking as its essential feature.

'Animism.' The spirit or soul that is involved in animism is a personal entity having the human characteristics of perception, feeling and thought and which is capable of action, producing effects in the physical world. Primitive peoples believed that all objects in nature have minds or souls and that natural forces are the work of their gods. Present day religions accept the term as meaning the existence of a soul in a material universe.

Divinities. Religion progresses from impersonal polytheism, through personal polytheism to personal monotheism, and terminates in impersonal monotheism. Belief in a single god is known as 'monotheism,' while belief in several divine beings is called 'polytheism,' and there are types of religion intermediate between these, known as 'dualisms.' In all religions that claim more than one divinity there is a difference in power among them, as well as a difference in the malevolent and benevolent functions of each. The history of various religions seems to bear out the fact that as a religion becomes older its divinities or divinity seem to become less personal.

Cosmos. Cosmos means the world or universe as an ordered whole, as an embodiment of order and harmony. Religions founded on this principle conceived their god as an impersonal force or system of laws or principle of reality underlying the universe.

Daimons. The term daimon applies properly to a supernatural person who is below the rank of divinity. Angels fall into this category, as do human souls and demons.

Mana or **Power.** The concept of mana is world-wide in religion. It was found in ancient religions; it is still prevalent among savages and is found in modern religions of civilized peoples. Belief in amulets, charms or holy relics as possessing certain powers or forms of protection falls in this category.

Souls. This is probably the most confused word in ancient and modern religions when attempts are made to define it. Its meaning seems to be different with every belief, and there are even different meanings within one cult. Several meanings attached to this appurtenance are: (a) the life principle or psyche; (b) the ego or subject of consciousness; (c) the personal daimon or guardian; (d) the ghost or image of a human being after death; (e) the in-dweller or external soul; (f) the immortal man himself.

Metamorphosis. This is a belief that a human being or god can be transformed into a lower animal or plant. This is not evident in current religions.

Sin. Probably all religions have some concept of sin, which is usually interpreted as meaning a violation or transgression of a religious or moral principle embodied in the particular religious belief, a violation of a part or parts of an established set of commandments con-tained in the religion.

Other World. While there are many different con-cepts of an 'other world' among the different religions, the commonly accepted belief is that the 'other world' is very sharply contrasted with the world of everyday life. It is usually regarded as the place where the dead are still existing and is conceived as the residence of the gods or of God and the angels. The 'other world' dis-tinguished between 'natural' and 'super-natural.' It is thought of as timeless and spaceless by the more pro-gressive religious beliefs.

Salvation. Salvation is generally considered as the process or the condition of 'being saved' or of being rescued from some harm, danger, risk or hazard. In some religions it is the person's 'soul' which is saved, either in this world or in an 'other world.'

Mystical Experience. Spiritual knowledge, indepen-dent of reasoning process, of truths believed to trans-cend ordinary understanding. The mystical experience is above all feeling as it is above knowledge. It is indescribable in words, a supernatural principle.

Holiness. Holiness is classified as pertaining to persons, places and to objects. It is the antithesis of sin. A holy person possesses mana or power; a holy place is a locality in which the power or mana of a god or a holy person is manifested. Holy objects possess this power or mana because of their possession or former possession of a holy person. In ancient and savage religions these manas could be producers of good or bad results; in modern religions they are beneficial only.

Divinities. In the evolution of divinities the gods were first conceived as trees or plants, then as animals, then finally took on gradually and by degrees the human form. The transition from animal divinities to divinities in human form is clearly recorded in the representations of the gods of the Egyptians where some had animal bodies with human heads and vice versa. Gods in animal and human form have always been endowed with sex, being first goddesses, then gods. The early gods moved about on earth much as men and animals do, but later they were believed to fly through the air, though not necessarily needing wings.

Religion, even in its late stages, is directed by desires. The activities of religion are accredited as means to the satisfaction of desires.

Symbolism

Symbolism has always been a vital and inherent factor in religious worship.

A symbol is an object, a pictorial design or an item of behavior that represents a concept of religion. Most of the symbols employed in modern religion are of great antiquity. The cross to Christians, the six-pointed star to Jews, the crescent to Mohammedans are well-known examples of religious symbols.

It appears that the rituals of worship have always been believed to be more effective and the benefits more certain if these rituals were conducted at the place where there was a symbolic representation of the divinity than if they were conducted elsewhere. Attending religious service in a building and a room prepared especially for this purpose assists the worshippers in attaining a worshipful attitude. The social contact with others who are there for the same purpose assists and strengthens the worshipful atmosphere.

In many religions, material objects ritually blessed, shrines and other holy places are not only symbols of religion but as a result of the "blessing" they are filled with manas, with special powers beneficial to those in possession of these objects or who present themselves to these places. It is also believed by many that the manas of symbols can be communicated to objects that come into contact with them or that are ritually associated with them.

Organization

Without organization no religion would survive. Organization is the life principle of religion. Without organization, social religion is impossible; and without social religion, personal religion would perish. The church is religon, organized and vitalized.

Organization of religion strengthens the cultural group in which religion is organized. Organized religion tends to unify the group and reduce the danger of disintegration.

An individual, then, who wishes to advance religious culture must do so through an organized group, for it is only through organized effort that progress can be made. The power expressed in unity is the only power that can advance toward higher standards.

Organized religion must be conservative, consistently so, clinging to the past, because the new must be proven before it can be accepted by a group, by an organization.

As to the future of religion in civilization, a religion may be expected to live only as long as it conforms to four conditions:

1. The doctrine or faith involved in the religion must be based on authority.

2. The doctrines of the sect must include a definite faith in another world, which other world for modern religion must be both the residence of divinity and the place in which the appurtenance of the human being that survives after death has its existence.

3. Faith that certain rituals are efficacious in human relations with the other world are useful in many stages of religious development.

4. The younger generations in the religious groups must be sedulously instructed in the doctrines of the sect and protected against secular influences that undermine faith.

Regardless of the group or the beliefs contained in its teachings, these four elements must remain basic or the particular religion will soon cease to exist.

5. A fifth should also be added. To live a religion must grow, it must be a missionary religion. It is a fundamental law of nature that anything which does not grow will soon die. A religion that does not possess the vitality

of growth, of the desire for winning others into its fold, does not possess the vitality for life. One reason for the continuing lack of unity of religions is that each considers its first duty to be that of converting the entire world to its particular belief because it believes its creed to be the only true one. But without this feeling of certainty within its tenets it would soon cease to believe in them and the entire organization would disintegrate.

Funerary Praxes and Rituals

Of all the cultural features of past ages, the practices of disposal of the bodies of the dead are of particular interest.

(a) Such practices are universally obligatory; every man dies, and at his death something must be done about his body.

(b) The disposal of a dead body is bound up with the emotional results of bereavement, with fears for the living as well as for the dead, with the system of family life, and with group integration. Funeral customs therefore have a significance for group life that few other customs have.

(c) Funeral customs are always parts of group religion.

(d) Although some of the less permanent products of religion have been lost from the ancients, those best known have been preserved in the ancient burial places.

The rituals evolved about the disposal of the dead are essential for the study of religion. The disposal of the deceased has taken a variety of forms.

(1) **Abandonment**. The most primitive tribes of mankind practiced abandonment. The tribe merely moved its campsite, leaving the dead body lay.

(2) **Exposure**. The body is taken to a place in the

forest where it is devoured by scavanger beasts, or it is thrown into a river or the sea, or set adrift at sea on a raft or in a specially constructed boat. Many peoples have observed these practices.

(3) **Cannibalism.** Many parts of the world have practiced cannibalism in the past. This practice was quite common in Europe before the Christian era.

(4) **Dismemberment and Mutilation.** Many primitive burial places have been unearthed where the bodies had been dismembered before burial, presumably to prevent it from returning to haunt the surviving. Others stripped the flesh from the bones and made separate disposals of the two parts. Egyptian mummification was partial dismemberment, since the organs of the body were removed as part of the mummification procedure.

(5) **Elevation.** The body was by some tribes placed in the crotch of a tree, by others on a specially constructed platform as high in the tree as possible and left for the scavenger birds. In most such instances the bones were later buried.

(6) **Cremation.** Cremation probably started with the burning of the deceased person's hut as soon as the individual died. Later, a funeral pyre was built and the body placed on that and burned. Some seafaring tribes placed the body on a boat, set the boat afire and set the boat adrift. Modern cremation in progressive countries is accomplished in specially constructed crematories and in a strictly sanitary manner.

Since cremation is misunderstood by so many people, a word of explanation here might be in order.

Cremation is not burning the body. The human body is about 90% water and, therefore, cannot burn.

Cremation is a process of evaporation. Just as a small burn on the skin of the body forms a blister because the extreme heat on that particular spot draws body water to the surface—we have all noted that a burned blister is always filled with water—just so the intense heat of cremation draws all of the body water to the surface and evaporates it. Since the body is composed of water and mineral matter, the latter being mostly in the bones, all that remains following cremation are a few pounds of mineral matter.

Incidentally, the correct term to be used is not 'ashes,' but 'cremated remains' or cremains.'

(7) **Burial.** Burial may be either interment in the ground or entombment in a mausoleum above the ground. Both of these may be individual or they might be prepared to contain several bodies.

In many parts of the world where burial is practiced and where the ground is scarce due to the dense population and many centuries of this practice, the bones of the decomposed bodies are removed from graves or tombs and other burials made in these same graves. The bones are disposed of in a common plot of ground where they have accumulated for centuries. In the more densely populated metropolitan areas of the United States, graves are often dug several graves deep. '

Earth burial, entombment and cremation have been practiced quite universally throughout the world, from the most ancient of times down to the present. The other forms have been found only among the primitive peoples of the world.

Man clings tenaciously to the customs of his forefathers, even if the sentiments that created them have become blunted and the rituals need new interpretations.

After Life. According to the studies of the many beliefs and religions from early times down to the present, the 'soul' or 'spirit' of the dead will experience at least one of four fates:

(1) It may hover around the place of burial or around its former abode or may pass to an underworld.

(2) It may go to the ancestral home of the group, which thus becomes the 'happy hunting ground,' the 'isles of the blest,' or 'paradise.'

(3) It may enter into some animal.

(4) It may become a free-living daimon, with no further essential connection with human beings.

Rituals persist after the beliefs in which they were formerly interpreted have been abandoned. Many persons do not believe that the rituals attending death and burial have any effect but they still approve the rituals. For these persons the rituals have ceased to be religious, but are merely conforming to established customs.

Conclusion

Because a funeral service is a religious service the funeral director must realize, as does the psychologist, that every religion is a spontaneous expression of a certain predominant psychological condition and that religion is a normal product of man's conscious processes, his desires, his fears, and especially his planning for future contingencies. The roles which religion has played in the cultures of the past are a basis for the evaluation of religion as to its nature and the roles which it may play in future civilization. Since religion is incontestably one of the earliest and most universal activities of the human mind, it is self-evident that any study of the psychological structure of human personality cannot avoid at least observing the fact that religion is not only a sociological or historical phenomenon, but also something of considerable personal concern to a great number of individuals.

Religion is not any particular creed. Creeds are codified and dogmatized forms of original religious experience. The contents of the experience have become sanctified and usually congealed in a rigid, often elaborate, structure. The practice and the reproduction of the original experience have become a ritual and an institution. The psychologist, inasmuch as he assumes a scientific attitude, has to disregard the claim of every creed to be the unique and eternal truth. He must be watchful of the human side of the religious problem. The life of the primitive individual is filled with constant regard for the ever-lurking possibility of physical dangers, and the attempts and procedures employed to diminish the risks are very numerous. There are numerous creeds and ceremonies that exist for the sole purpose of forming a defense against the unexpected and the unknown.

Religion that has the greatest value does not emphasize simply the existence of a providence that is beneficent, but of a providence that gives strength to achieve a fuller life, and hence courage and initiative. Religion should strengthen, as well as comfort man. Religion that develops not a passive attitude toward most problems of life, but an aspiring and rational attitude towards problems within one's power of solution, may be a most potent factor in the furtherance of security.

Man is the only living organism that has given any evidence of religious thought, making religion uniquely human. Religious study is totally a study of humans. There is evidence of religious activity among mankind as far back as records have been found. Mankind evidently has always believed in a higher power. He has sought protection, guidance and favors from this higher power. He has given this higher power the emotions of his own nature: love, hate, vengeance, sorrow, repentance, joy, forgiveness. He has done this because man's mind is capable of creating and understanding only the things he himself can experience. He has called his gods spiritual but he has made them human with powers above his own. The superman idea has always been in man's mind, long before there was a fictional character by that name. That was man's only explanation of events beyond his comprehension and control. The things man could not understand and control he laid at the feet of his gods, making them responsible.

This fear of superhuman retribution and punishment for misdeeds has been a powerful force in causing man to "behave" as the customs of his people and his "conscience" have dictated. Without such fear it is quite likely the world would be more chaotic than it is.

While it is true many people turn to "religion" at times of death, many do so because it is the accepted thing, and not for religious reasons. The religious ritual, therefore, is not always motivated by faith or comfort, per se, but by socio-phychological factors that are even more powerful in causing people to conform.

The religious service provides a release of tension; it is a great comfort to those in grief. Even the simplest funeral service is a ritual acknowledging certain fundamental needs in the minds of the survivors. When the funeral director fully understands this and when he fully understands the meaning of such service for the bereaved family and friends, each service he plans and conducts will assume a richer meaning and a most important role in his attempt to serve his clients to their complete satisfaction.

The challenge to funeral directors is that of their meaningful and unfaltering support of the religious organization of their choice in their respective communities, with the realization that it is these symbols of religious faith that are the very bulwarks of all that is held sacred in our civilization today, that if these institutions fall, serious consequences will follow.

In his service to his clients the funeral director will sincerely exert every effort to plan and conduct every service he has so that the utmost of comfort and solace will come to each griefstricken individual from the religious part of the service as well as from his skill in restoring lifelike appearance to the beloved body itself. There can be no greater service to mankind than such a challenge properly met.

There is also a further challenge to all funeral directors. Such challenge is probably best understood under the category of the word "tolerance." But it goes much deeper than a mere statement that one should be tolerant of other persons' religious beliefs and customs.

Merely to "tolerate" viewpoints different from one's own is far from the true meaning of friendship, service and neighborliness.

There are those who "make light" of minority groups who practice customs differing from those of the great majority. To make fun or to look askance at another because of his sincere religious observance is to not be worthy of being allowed to follow one's own choice of religion. One must not merely "live and let live" but must "live and help live." As the world is being made smaller by improved means of transportation and communication, it is becoming more and more imperative that all peoples of the earth not only permit all others freedom of religion, but to sincerely assist them in such observance when it falls to the lot of one, such as the funeral director, to arrange such service or to assist in any way. To belittle another person's belief or ritual because it is different from his own, or because such observance dictates use of low quality merchandise and service is for a man not to be worthy of the term professional servant, be he funeral director or other professional or business man.

Let all men be worthy of the classification "human being" by practicing conscientiously any one of the Golden Rules listed in the forepart of this chapter as the universal rule of all mankind. Let us add another rule of life: "Do not belittle another man's religious belief."

Voltaire has been credited with saying: "I do not believe a thing you say, but I will defend with my life your right to say it."

No man dares to do less than that, for such is the very foundation of all freedom.

Funeral Procedure

There are several hundred religious denominations, ranging in size from one congregation of a few persons to denominations of several thousand congregations totaling several million members. There are also many fraternal groups that perform a funeral ceremony upon request, the principle of which has come down to us from the medieval guilds wherein it was mandatory that every brother accompany the departed to his last resting place. The funeral director recognizes and cooperates with all of these groups that may be in his community. He should be familiar with the customs and practices of these groups in their funeral observances.

LOCAL CUSTOM must prevail in every instance. However, many of these denominations and fraternal orders do have certain specified observances or rituals that must be observed. The funeral director must have knowledge of these if he is to properly serve the families who are members of these denominations and orders.

First of all, the funeral director should notify the clergy of the church to which the deceased belonged as soon after death as possible, if this has not already been done by a member of the family or someone else. This also should be done, as a courtesy, to the head officer or secretary of any fraternal order or trade union to which the deceased belonged.

There are a few churches that require the priest to be present at the time of death, if this is possible. These include the Eastern Orthodox, Roman Catholic, Protestant Episcopal, Holy Orthodox, American Orthodox, Syrian Antiochian Orthodox and Ukranian Orthodox.

There are many requirements, prohibitions and preferences of certain denominations regarding funeral services and final disposal of the body that should be familiar to the funeral director.

Cremation is prohibited by the Eastern Orthodox, Greek Orthodox, Holy Orthodox, Independent Fundamental, American Orthodox, Rabinnical Council of America, Romanian Orthodox, Russian Orthodox and Ukranian Orthodox. The Rabinnical Council of America (Orthodox Jews) goes further in that it requires earth burial, prohibiting mausoleum interment.

Cremation is discouraged by the Christian Reformed,

Church of Jesus Christ of Latter Day Saints (Mormon), Pentecostal, Foursquare, American Hebrew, Evangelical Lutheran, Norwegian Lutheran Menonite and Wesleyan Methodist. On the other hand, cremation is preferred by the Buddhist and is required by the I Am group, the last mentioned specifying that the body be cremated on the third day after death.

Embalming is forbidden by the Orthodox Jews and the I Am group.

Funeral services are required to be held in the church by the Eastern Orthodox, Roman Catholic, Greek Orthodox, Holy Orthodox, American Orthodox, Russian Orthodox and Ukranian Orthodox. Service in the church is preferred by the Church of Jesus Christ of Latter Day Saints (Mormon), Protestant Episcopal, all Lutheran groups, Wesleyan Methodist, Moravian Church in America, Pentecostal Holiness and Syrian Antiochian Orthodox. On the other hand, funeral service in the mortuary chapel is preferred by the Christian Science, American Hebrew (Reformed Jew) and the Rabinnical Council of America (Orthodox Jew). The last named prefer the home over the mortuary chapel.

Flowers are not permitted in the church at a funeral for Rabinnical Council of America and Syrian Antiochian Orthodox. Other individual ministers discourage flowers. Many Protestant Episcopal churches prohibit flowers being brought into the church.

No music is permitted in funeral services of the Eastern Orthodox or Ukranian Orthodox.

A closed casket is specified by the Free Will Baptist during the service, Roman Catholic for laymen and nuns but open for a priest, Protestant Episcopal, American Hebrew (Reformed Jew) preferred, Holy Orthodox, all

Lutheran preferred, American Orthodox, Rabinnical Council of America (Orthodox Jew), Syrian Antiochian Orthodox. Some denominations specify an open casket, the Advent General Conference, Buddhist, Pentecostal, Greek Orthodox, Holy Orthodox, Romanian Orthodox and Russian Orthodox.

The body is ritualistically dressed by the Eastern Orthodox, Church of Jesus Christ of Latter Day Saints (Mormon) and the Babinnical Council of America (Orthodox Jew).

As to the fraternal groups, the ritual is religious in nature, usually, and can be used in any funeral service if permitted by the particular church in charge.

Sometimes a fraternal service will be conducted the evening before the religious service. Only one fraternal group has any specific regulation or requirement as to its service. The Masons must conduct their service last and perform the final commitment at the cemetery or the crematory. If Masonic service is conducted, all other services, religious or fraternal, must be held previous to the Masonic. Many of the grand lodges of Masons require that all active bearers be Masons, but each grand lodge is autonomous.

Controversial matters such as might arise between a clergyman and a fraternal order can be settled only by the next of kin. Since some churches will not permit their ministers to participate in a funeral service where a fraternal order has a part, only the family of the deceased can decide which one is to conduct the service. Some funeral services are conducted by a fraternal group only, with no clergyman officiating at all.

There are other customs that do not pertain to the religious or fraternal groups, but are regional. One of these is the custom of evening viewings. In the eastern, midwestern, southern and some parts of the western section of the United States, it is the custom to hold evening viewings. The family of the deceased will spend the evening prior to the day of the funeral service at the mortuary or home where friends will call to view the deceased, to pay their respects. Much of the western area does not observe this custom. The custom is a holdover of the wake that used to be universally observed. Where the custom of the evening viewing is observed, the attendance here is often much larger than the attendance at the funeral service.

Funeral arrangements should never be completed by the funeral director and family without consultation with the clergyman who is to officiate as to the time and place of the service. In polls taken among ministers this is the most common complaint by them against funeral directors, that the time of the funeral is decided without consultation with the clergyman in charge.

In a very real sense, the clergyman and the funeral director are partners in a service which is basically religious. They work in partnership to alleviate the grief and suffering of bereaved families. Between them they have developed a religious, social, sentimental and practical service that mankind appreciates and needs in its darkest hours.

(NOTE:—The material in this portion that relates to definite denominational practices and procedures is taken from the book, Manual of Funeral Procedures, by permission of the author John M. Myers.)

CHAPTER X

PUBLIC RELATIONS

Its Importance

The public relations of the mortician, as with every individual who serves the public in any manner, is everything he does and everything he says, not only while he is on duty but all of the time. Every contact with another individual makes an impression. If that impression is favorable, then the public relations program is good; if that impression is unfavorable, then the public relations program is not good. This applies to every employee of the firm and every member of every family connected with the firm. It is necessary to be genuinely interested in people in every contact with them, not merely while serving them in a business or professional way.

Due to the fact that the funeral director's services to his families are so intimate and so sacred there seems to be more expected of him in the element of personal character integrity than of many other business or professional men of the community. Other professional men are chosen more for their ability than for any other quality. For example, a doctor whose reputation for skill is unequalled will be called, regardless of his friendliness. The same is true of a lawyer or a dentist. People patronize a certain store because of its unmatched values in merchandise or the size of its stock or any one of many other reasons. But when it comes to selecting a funeral director to serve a family in their time of sorrow, to care for the body of a father or mother or son or daughter, this family wants a man in whom they have the utmost confidence, not only for his skill but for his integrity, his honesty, his high standard of service, his moral character. They do not want to entrust the body, which is sacred to them, into the hands of a man whom they can not freely trust to care for it with the utmost reverence. In the great emotional upset they are experiencing they are entirely dependent upon him to guide them in arranging a service that will serve as a fitting and proper memorial to the memory of the life that is gone. There must be no doubt in their minds about these factors in the funeral director in whom they place this trust. These factors are much more pronounced in small communities than in large cities because of the daily contact of the funeral director with the people of his community.

When death invades the home it brings tragedy, shock, loss, heartache, bewilderment; and it stirs emotional impulses which seek expression. So far as the funeral profession has succeeded in meeting that situation, so far as it has been able to soften the shock, assuage the heartache, satisfy emotional groping, supply counsel and assume responsibilities which relieve the bewilderment, it has certainly found favor with the public.

It is difficult to be suddenly separated from that which is greatly valued. People wish to have the opportunity to bid an appropriate farewell to one whose life has intimately touched their own, which explains why families hold memorial services in memory of loved ones who are killed overseas during a war. It is human nature to buttress inner consciousness by outward evidence of devotion. People are influenced by the desire to do that which meets the approval of others, to plan according to established custom. This motive possessing important social significance, eases their tension.

The refinements of modern funeral service, its personal and professional aspects, its well-planned buildings and facilities, its reposing state-rooms, chapels, coaches, caskets, flowers, music, ceremony, are prompted by those it is set up to serve.

The funeral service profession exists only because it has received the approval of the public. This approval indicates that people look upon the ceremony of laying away the dead as a significant one, entitled to be conducted with appropriate regard for the memory of the deceased and for the sake of the living.

American Standards

The difference between the funeral customs in most of the world and those followed for the most part on the North American continent, which the American people have accepted, is the service which the funeral director renders to the families he serves. All of that service is aimed at rendering a service for the living, not a service for the dead. This attitude explains the difference between the high standards attained by the American funeral director, now being followed in more advanced parts of the world, and the customs still practiced throughout most of the world today. For example, according to our standards, embalming the dead body is done for three principle reasons: (a) sanitation and the prevention of the spread of disease; (b) preservation, particularly for the period between death and final disposition; (c) cosmetic effect to restore lifelike appearance, thus comforting the bereaved.

A concise statement which explains quite well the typical attitude of the American standard of funeral service was expressed by a successful funeral director as follows: "We evaluate every policy, every service and every piece of merchandise which we sell to the public of our community on a basis of increased satisfaction to the family and friends of the deceased. The application of that principle on every service we render forces us to treat every family as if they were our own, every body as though it were a member of our own family. On that basis every member of the firm and every one of our employees is a sincere believer in the value of the service we render to the people of our community, thereby making every one of them a better, more sincere salesman for our firm."

It is a great comfort to any family to have their friends say to them after the service is over, "You certainly did everything possible for your mother. I never saw anyone laid away more beautifully. The service was lovely." Public approval means much to the bereaved family. Every funeral director should keep this fact in mind from the time he answers the first call until the service is completed.

Aside from the actual embalming for reasons of sanitation, every bit of service rendered by the embalmer and funeral director is done for psychological reasons. And even the sanitation phase has psychological repercussions, for the public expects it.

Every embalmer and funeral director is essentially two people. First, he is a professional man and technician, and must therefore be highly trained and competent. Second, he is a human being and a citizen and must therefore be a cultivated man, able to meet on equal terms with other professional men of his community. This implies an education broader than mere technical details. The desire to become professional must come from within the man himself, however, for it is an attitude of mind and a fundamental principle.

What Public Relations Is

Public relations can not be made anything different or separate for either emblaming or funeral directing. It is impossible to separate public relations from either of the professional or business phases of our vocation. Public relations is an integral part of every phase of our service, from the first call to the final disposition of the body. It is a part of everything we do between those calls for service. It is a part of our conversation with friends as we meet them on the street, at church, at lodge. It is a part of the way our cars are driven down the street, whether by an employee or the owner. It is the attitude of the individual throughout the twenty-four hours of the day.

Public relations means more, then, than the manner of serving during the actual service and preparation for it. It means our behavior, reputation, character in everyday life, and our qualifications for our responsibilities. Public relations covers all those things that cause our friends to have confidence that we are qualified to serve them, and that we are the character of person to whom they can entrust the sacred dead of their household.

Public relations must stamp a funeral director as

suitable and successful before he can receive that first call for service. A poet said, "It takes a heap of living in a house to make it home." This can be easily paraphrased to say it takes a heap of right living in a community to cause the public to believe a funeral director is the proper person to serve them profession-ally. It takes time to become established and favorably known.

Public relations for a businessman is the act of doing business with people. Public relations for a pro-fessional man is the act of serving people. The mortician is both a businessman and a professional man. His public relations program, however, can not be limited to the acts of doing business and serving people. The reason for this has already been explained. His public relations is everything he does and everything he says.

Good Will Essential

Good will is the most important factor in any vocation. It is the foundation upon which public ac-ceptance of a business or a profession is based. The most dangerous phase of any business or professional man's career is when he considers himself a success and does not feel so dependent on public good will. At this point his public relations program is headed for disaster. In some respects it is harder to maintain a successful reputation than it is to establish it because of the temptation to become careless in bidding for public good will. It is a law of Nature that everything must move, either forward or backward. A living thing that does not grow will soon die. A successful business or professional man must either continue to become more successful or he will become less successful. Without public good-will no man can long continue, no matter how successful he has become.

Public relations for the mortuary is designed to give it a good reputation with the public, establish it in the public mind as an institution of character and an institution which functions in the public interest.

Every funeral director should keep constant vigilance to see there are no "leaks" to impair the good opinion the community has always had of him and his establishment. The definite areas where unfavorable opinion may breed, that can be described as trouble-makers of all organizations, are: brusque telephone voice or manner, individual who is unpopular in his social life, a driver of the mortuary cars who "hogs" the road, curt business letters, lack of personal neatness among members of the firm, gloomy physical surroundings, lack of genuine and sincere interest in helping clients, referring clients from one person to another, inaccessible proprietor or official, failure to reply to or attempt to adjust complaints, disinterest in community enterprises, any attitude of carelessness or indifference, mechanical attitude in dealings with clients, and any number of other phases of the many details that are a part of a funeral director's life.

Most Important Features

The most important features of a funeral director's public relations program are to be found in the list compiled by the National Selected Morticians organization through a follow-up system maintained through its members with families served by those NSM members. In response to the question, "What one thing made the most favorable impression?" the families served listed the most important as follows:

> Personal attention
> Courtesy
> Good embalming
> Attention to all details
> Dignity
> Promptness

A survey by the same organization showed that from 70 to 75 percent of the reasons for preference of the mortuary chosen were founded upon:

> Previous service observation
> Reputation
> Recommendations

Public Relations begins at home, with the funeral director himself. There is no magic formula. It requires attention and work, and it must be done by the funeral director himself; no one else can do it for him. He must be pleasant and natural, he must always have patience with his people, always have time to give them proper service and attention, be courteous with everyone. There are a few necessary and essential factors.

Since three-fourths of the calls come to a mortuary, according to replies from the people themselves, because of past services performed, doesn't it prove that the services rendered today are by far the largest determining factor in the calls that are to be received in the future? On this basis it is easy to see how important it is for the funeral director to watch what he does and how he does it. His attention to details, his poise, his helpfulness and sympathetic attendance to the wants of the families he serves, these are the things the public observes and talks about. These factors are more important than the type of motor equipment or the funeral home maintained. The mortician's acceptance in his community is also indicated by community responsibilities, civic activities, organization activities. He must be a part of the community enterprise. Hence, it is the individual funeral director himself that determines his degrees of success in his community.

The Important "Little Things"

It might be well to briefly consider many of the practical phases of funeral service and the way they are performed that will influence the public for or against an individual funeral director. With this in mind it must be remembered that it is the so-called "little things" of funeral service that are the really important things. And it is these things that do more to determine success or failure in an individual than might be realized. Someone once said "The big things you can see with one eye closed, but keep both eyes wide open for the little things. Little things mark the great dividing line between success and failure." Since these small acts of thoughtfulness are so important, let us consider them as they contribute to making or marring the totality of professional funeral service.

Answering the Telephone

First of all, the way in which the telephone is answered is very important. This is the first contact between the mortuary and the family to be served. First impressions are in many respects the most important impressions of the whole procedure. The voice of the person answering is the only representative of the funeral establishment to the person doing the calling. This voice should be calm, pleasant, kindly, clear, sympathetic, should have those qualities that will soothe the upset nerves of a member of the family that might be calling. Imagine the shock if the voice is gruff and short, sounding perhaps as though the person answering the phone is inconvenienced by the call. Even when a doctor or a nurse does the calling this would be poor advertising. This very thing happens in too many mortuaries.

Every individual who serves the public should make a recording of his or her voice and then listen to it. This recording can give a person impressions about his voice that he can get in no other way and will probably reveal qualities of which he is completely unaware. The recording can serve as an invaluable device for making improvements, because quite often defects cannot be accurately and explicitly described by anyone offering suggestions or criticisms. It isn't so much that "even your best friend won't tell you," but rather that "even your best friend can't tell you."

Many aspects of voice and speech are important in personality because they are the means by which others judge an individual. Loud and raucous voices have always been associated with people who are on the whole undesirable. Sensitive persons are embarrassed when some member of their group speaks loudly enough to attract attention in a public place. Such a voice is inexcusable in a person associated with a funeral service establishment. Softness and restraint in conversational speech have long been associated with gentility, with well-mannered persons. By softness and restraint is meant controlled volume, not speech so low in volume that one's listeners can barely hear it.

Indistinct or otherwise disagreeable speech is a personality liability. A common cause of indistinctness is usually caused by the speaker not opening his mouth wide enough when speaking.

Incorrect pronunciation is another common fault

of speech.

For the human being, speech is the most important agency of social adaptation. It is a significant aspect of personality.

It is well for an individual to check his own speech delivery, preferably by means of a recording, and to note the following delivery factors: pitch (too high or too low, monotonous inflection or sing-song), volume (too much or too little), quality (harsh, nasal, thin, flat), tempo (too rapid, too slow, clipped or drawled, too long or too short pauses), articulation (pronunciation of words), mannerisms (clearing throat too frequently, emits "uh," "and uh," "ah" between phrases and sentences).

The manner of speech, the voice of the person answering a mortuary telephone is one of the most important phases of public relations and its importance can not be overemphasized.

Telephone Etiquette

Since, in the majority of instances following a death, the first contact with a family begins with a telephone conversation, and since this is so important a part of the public relations program of every mortuary, the following several paragraphs are quoted from material prepared by the Public Relations Department of the Bell Telephone Company and revised by them for the benefit of funeral directors:

"In perhaps no other business are tact and courtesy so important as in the business of the funeral director. The emotional strain under which the customer may be laboring when he has occasion to enlist the services of a funeral director, and the solemnity of funeral arrangements combine to provide an opportunity for the slightest lack of courtesy to be magnified to the extent of wounding deeply.

"In creating and maintaining an impression which inspires confidence, every telephone contact is important.

"In any business the wisdom of handling telephone calls properly is borne out by frequently-heard statements such as this:

" 'The Such and Such Company are good people to deal with. I've never been there but I have talked with them by telephone.'

"Indeed, to those who call your Company, the voice that comes back over the wire **is** the Company. And with each telephone conversation, the Company makes an impression, good, bad or indifferent. If your tone is gruff, the person at the other end of the line is apt to get the impression that 'that outfit' is rather unpleasant to deal with.

"Yes, the telephone voice of your company, whether it be a funeral home or a hardware store, is important in making and holding friends. And every employee who meets the public by telephone is a part of his company's telephone voice and its personality.

"Telephone personality—how you impress those with whom you talk—is composed of **What you say, How you say it, and Your Telephone Etiquette.**

"What you say to the customer over the telephone differs little from what you would say if face to face. Therefore, we shall consider **what** you say, only to the extent of mentioning that the use of good English is more important over the telephone than in a face-to-face conversation, and that little courtesy phrases such as 'Thank you,' 'You're welcome' and 'I'm sorry' and frequent use of the caller's name put a spirit of friendly personal interest in your conversation which pays good-impression dividends.

"What you **don't** say is often of great importance too. People like a good listener and dislike someone who is always interrupting.

"**How** you say it is definitely a part of telephone personality. Of first importance is clarity. If difficult to understand over the telephone there are 'two strikes on you before you go to bat.' And it should be remembered that a voice is less easily understood without the benefit of lip movements and facial expressions to read. To avoid being misunderstood, you should speak unhurriedly, though not slowly enough to be dull and uninteresting, directly into the telephone mouthpiece. Then it will not be necessary to shout; conversational tone is loud enough and infinitely more pleasing. Being understood also depends on distinct enunciation.

"It is well to remember that people will hesitate to call a person whom they must frequently interrupt with 'I didn't get that,' in order to understand him.

"Next to clarity, the most important part of **how** you say it is your **tone** of voice. There is a tendency to talk at the telephone and allow the voice to become mechanical, cold, expressionless. Visualizing a person at the other end of the line and speaking to him and not at the telephone will help put more life into your voice.

"By proper inflection, rising and falling of the voice, and emphasis, the voice can convey a smile, a handshake and the other gestures characteristic of a pleasing personality, and express a desire to be helpful. This quality can be cultivated. In our business it's called 'The Voice With a Smile.'

"Even a person who knows what to say and how to say it may ruin the impression by thoughtless telephone etiquette.

"On first thought, how you answer the telephone, how you handle the conversation, and how you hang up the receiver may seem of little consequence. With a little more thought, though, you may recall how somebody made you angry when you got a 'wrong number'; how you impatiently said to yourself 'Everybody must be dead over there' when the phone was allowed to ring and ring before anyone answered; or the time when someone carelessly slammed down the receiver before it became clear that the conversation was ended. Remember how angry you were, how you said aloud, 'What's that guy trying to do, burst my eardrum?'

"People do notice faulty telephone usage and discourtesy. Some react very strongly. . . ."

This material goes on to emphasize the importance of common courtesy in telephone etiquette. The first rule of telephone manners, it says, is to answer the telephone **promptly**. The longer the telephone is allowed to ring before it is answered the more impatient the caller becomes. "Answering the telephone is given priority" usually. "Excusing oneself, if necessary, long enough to take the caller's name and telephone number for a return call may be done gracefully."

It is necessary to identify yourself when answering the telephone. " 'Hello,' 'All right,' or 'Yes' as a means of greeting a telephone caller . . . are just about as useful as a grunt." Such an answer requires that questions be asked by the person calling in order to learn if he has the right number or the person wanted. The telephone greeting should tell the caller at once that he has reached the right telephone and who is answering.

Speak **distinctly**, always. ". . . . a mouth full of cigar, chewing gum or pencil is not particularly conducive to distinct speech. Holding the telephone properly in front of the mouth, on the other hand, does help make your speaking clear."

Be prepared. Never keep the caller waiting longer than is absolutely necessary. "If it becomes necessary to leave the telephone to obtain information, courtesy says tell the caller how long it will take and ask him whether he had rather wait or have you call back."

If the person asked for is out, the person who answers should say, "Mr. Jones is out until 1:30. May I help you or shall I have him call you when he returns?" This expresses a friendly desire to **be helpful**.

When a conversation has been ended, pleasantly say "Goodbye" or "Thank you." "Slamming the receiver without taking leave is on a par with slamming the door in a visitor's face."

This article emphasizes throughout, the importance of **a pleasant voice**. "Your telephone personality is measured by how you impress those with whom you talk. It is a direct result of what you say and how you say it.

"The practice of good telephone etiquette by every-one who answers calls will help further establish your company in the public mind as a courteous, friendly and helpful organization worthy of confidence and patronage.

"People prefer to do business with places where their contacts are **pleasant**."

While the telephone voice is extremely important, we must not lose sight of the importance of voice quali-ties at other times, also. Holmes has said, "Talking is one of the fine arts—the noblest, the most important, the most difficult—and its fluent harmonies may be spoiled by the intrusion of a single harsh note."

Speech is a tool of social adjustment, a psychological and sociological technique of modifying human responses by means of thought, language, voice and action; and it is an indication of personality integration.

Your Speaking Voice

Good speech is important, because when one speaks he reveals his environment, disposition, personality, mental alertness, health and breeding. The impression he makes on his associates is largely determined by the quality of the voice and diction used.

Some authorities estimate that there are more than ten million speech cripples in our country, including stutterers and persons with bad speech defects due to pathological or psychological disturbances, sickness or operations, but aside from these serious cases there are many millions more whose speech defects consist merely of tonal unpleasantness or bad habits traceable to environment, disposition or character. Not more than five out of every hundred people have a really good speaking voice, yet many times that number need a good voice in earning their livelihood.

A recent survey showed the following bad speech habits are prominent reasons given for failures of employees to advance: Shrill, nasal or raucous voice; stuttering; sing-song replies, especially on the telephone; sharp retorts, baby-talk, and garrulousness. In addition to these defects many others could be listed, such as guttural, high-pitched, squeaky, monotonous, husky, whispering, metallic, coarse, flat, growling, hard, harsh, muffled, passive, rasping, rough, sepulchral, sombre, strident and toneless. There are yet dozens of other irritating ways of talking, such as stilted, stumbling, rambling, repetitive, colloquial, over-friendly, sarcastic, cynical, slobbery, affected, hesitating and labored.

There are also several physical actions accompanying speech which also cause antagonism or annoyance in listeners. Among these are sputtering, grabbing a listener's arm or tapping his chest, talking while eating, using outlandish gestures, stroking the face or scratching the head and looking away from the person addressed.

Monopolizing a conversation is often a sign of an inferiority complex. Frequently it reveals a determination to gain attention which would not be forthcoming if the speaker were less insistent. At best, monopolizing a conversation is bad manners.

To improve one's speech a few suggestions might be offered. Keep healthy and try to remedy any physical defects affecting the speech. The disposition is clearly reflected in the voice; therefore, anything that can be done to improve it, from eating sensibly to controlling the temper, will help the speech. Relaxation is the first step in curing speech ailments.

Good Impression Through Speech

The mortician must give the same good impression by his manner of speaking as he attempts to do through the other means of public contact. He should be calm and reassuring. **Attitudes are contagious.** A funeral director who is conservative and unhurried in speech and actions creates an atmosphere that will help the emotionally upset family he is serving to become more quiet and collected. He should maintain sufficient reserve and dignity to beget confidence and at the same time understand their feelings so that he can say the right things at the right time. He must maintain the respect and confidence of those he serves, of those he contacts.

Terminology

There is one thing that seems almost too trivial to mention, and that is the terminology used in speaking of the various phases of funeral service. Serious errors are not apt to be made by the funeral directors themselves, but some apprentice or young person or some inexperienced person working in the mortuary can easily do a vast amount of harm to a well-established firm by talking too much and by using the wrong terminology. First of all, of course, topics relating to the funeral profession should be avoided as much as possible. It is not a proper topic of conversation, and to many people within hearing of such conversation it is repulsive.

The following are suggested as proper terms:

Service, not funeral

Mr., Mrs., Miss Blank, not corpse or body

Preparation room, not morgue

Casket, not coffin

Funeral director or mortician, not undertaker

Reposing room or slumber room, not laying-out room

Selection room, not showroom

Baby or infant, not stillborn

Deceased, not dead

Autopsy or post-mortem, not post

Casket coach, not hearse

Shipping case, not shipping box

Flower car, not flower truck

Cremains, or cremated remains, not ashes

Clothing, dress, suit, etc., not shroud

Drawing room, not parlor

The use of improper terminology by anyone affiliated with a mortuary should be strictly forbidden. Respect, yes, even reverence, is the attitude of the bereaved family toward their own deceased. The attitude of everyone having any part in the care of these same deceased can not, then, be any less thoughtful.

Proper Dress and Posture

Not only the language, but also the appearance of everyone of the personnel of a mortuary who contacts the public must be neat and clean, not only for the sake of general appearance, but for the sake of sanitation and of maintaining the proper sentiment and attitude toward the work they are doing and the people they are serving.

Good posture is a decided personality asset and is essential to the best public relations. An erect posture and a graceful gait may have nothing to do with a person's ability in general, but they are a distinct aid in giving others a good general impression. Posture can be the deciding factor in favor of or against an individual funeral director if he is a stranger to a person evaluating him. Posture influences others in their evaluation of one's personality.

Just as listening to one's own voice is valuable in correcting speech faults, so watching a motion picture of one's self is important in analyzing posture, gait and form. Actually seeing one's self as others see him is of much more value than having another describe his actions to him. When one can see faults in his posture the matter of making the proper adjustments or improvements becomes very simple, usually. If a funeral director could see a motion picture of himself throughout his direction of a funeral he might be amazed at some of his motions, things he does of which he is not aware, wasted movements, awkward poses, ungainly posture. Real help in overcoming some posture defect is already under way when the defect is recognized.

Service Attitude

In addition to the personality traits of the individual there are many things to consider in the way in which the funeral director serves his families, his attitude toward them. These are the elements of his service, the things that are under direct and immediate control.

The First Call

The mortician's first opportunity for service comes with the death call. Some family has just suffered the worst kind of tragedy—one of their loved ones has died. They have just suffered a loss that is irreplaceable. There is lost hope in this loss. They have that helpless feeling that has no adequate physical outlet. They have called their chosen mortician because they have confidence that he can, through his service, cause this tragic experience to be just a little easier to bear, that he can cause the memory of this loss to be just as much of a comfort to them as it is possible to make it. It is his personal service they are needing—the merchandise is incidental. A casket can be purchased from any mortuary, but this particular funeral director is called because it is his service they need. He is, therefore, a professional man—

he serves.

On this first opportunity for service to this family his first obligation is **promptness**. Every five minutes seems like an hour to the waiting grief-stricken family. Their feelings are on edge; they are easily irritated. He is expected to be ready to respond to a call immediately at any time. They may have waited an hour or more for members of the family to arrive at the bedside, but when the funeral director is called he is expected to come promptly.

There is one feature of the first call that may seem too trivial to mention, even embarrassing to think about. That is the matter of always using clean linen on every call. To cite a specific example of the feeling of many persons on this, a nurse once said, "Can you imagine a funeral director making a first call with soiled linen? Well, there are some in this city who do, and I would not let them touch a member of my family, just for that reason." She then mentioned by name the largest firm in that city and said, "I don't care how much the other firms criticize this firm, their linen is always immaculate, they are always quiet and dignified when they make a call, and any time I have the opportunity to call a mortician they will always be my choice. I know nothing else about them except that they do the most business in the city. The one and only request I have made regarding myself when I die is that clean linen be used when the mortician comes for my body. Every nurse in this large hospital feels the same as I do." This statement by this nurse explained the exact reason for the preference on the part of many nurses for this particular mortuary.

This nurse proceeded to quote specific instances of

crudeness and carelessness on the part of some of the small operators in her city, instances that were actually revolting. These small firms probably wondered why one particular mortuary in their city received the most of the death calls. They did the common thing, psychologically—applied a defense reaction, instead of intelligently analyzing the situation with careful scrutiny. By the psychological mechanism of displacement they heaped the blame on their largest competitor by accusing him of being unethical instead of "looking into the mirror" and attempting to learn where they themselves might possibly be at fault.

Another feature of the first call that means more to a grief-stricken family than we might realize is the manner in which the body is removed from the bed in the home or the hospital to the mortician's first-call bed. The most tender care that can be used at this time means much, in the attitude of those witnessing these actions, toward the firm making the call. Again, the words of a nurse will be quoted. She said, "Mr. (Mortician), I noticed the way you removed the body of Mrs. Blank from the hospital bed. You did it as though she were a sick person instead of being dead. You do not seem to be hardened to such incidents as we often think you morticians get from being so used to your work." Many nurses frequently speak in very uncomplimentary terms of the loud talking and the noise made by some attendants in calling for bodies of deceased persons.

If these things are so noticeable to nurses who are accustomed to such work, think how much more little attentions and thoughtful acts and care mean to members of the family when they witness them. If the first-call attendants become accustomed to exercising thoughtful care at all times in this phase of their service, it will become the natural way for them to act, and there can then be no occasion for criticism on the part of any observer, whether it be a member of the family, a nurse, a doctor, or some family friend present. It is the same thought as is used by a mother in teaching a child good manners. If the child is always accustomed to performing properly, then there is no need for the mother to have fear of the proper performance of the child in the presence of any company at any time. The deceased body is sacred to the members of the family and must be so treated by all attendants.

Another important phase of the first call is the personnel involved. It is good psychology, good public relations, especially in the smaller firms, where the volume is not too large, for the owner himself to go on every call. One funeral director in a large city doing a large volume of business, making it impossible for him to go on many of the first calls, made it a point to contact every family himself in some way at some time between the first call and the final disposition, if it were only to inquire of the family if they were being taken care of to their satisfaction and if everything was all right.

Personal Service

Little attentions mean more to the grief-stricken than we may realize, for they feel helpless. Little things are greatly magnified in their minds. To them, their particular bereavement is the most important thing in the world at this time and **must** receive the undivided attention of those serving them.

The family must be made to feel that whatever service they need in the way of personal attention is theirs for the asking, if it has not already been attended to before they ask it. There are many things to do and they are not familiar with the proceedings. There are telegrams to send, notices to put in the papers, the clergy or the lodge to contact, place of service and burial to decide, and so many things that the funeral director can help the family arrange. His careful, kindly attention at this time takes the burdensome feeling off their minds. Some families wish to attend to the details themselves and thus keep their minds occupied, but the funeral director is always available for help when needed. He may not always do as much as the family thinks he is doing, but it is his helpful guidance that they appreciate in knowing they are proceeding as they should. Funeral arrangements are unfamiliar to them and his suggestions mean much.

What to Say and Do?

Many little problems become quite perplexing to funeral directors, so much so that often times they are at a loss as to the proper thing to do or to say. One successful funeral director asked the question of those present in a discussion group: "What shall we say when we go into the house on the first call? What are the first words we should speak to the family?" He went on to relate an experience that he had on one call to serve a friend who had lost his wife. The friend, he related, was deeply grieved. This funeral director gripped his friend by the hand and said, "Lew, I'm sorry." The friend turned around and said, "Why are you sorry? I do not want your sympathy because you are here on business." The grief-stricken man thought the funeral director was not sincere. The funeral director went on, "I have gotten to the point where I do not know what to say. I am more likely to take a person by the hand, hold it and give it a tight squeeze than I am to say anything."

The first question that arises in the student's mind, in fact, in the minds of all who are in their early experiences in serving grief-stricken families, is, "Just how much should the funeral director sympathize with his client?"

There can be no set rule, because everyone, including funeral directors, is different. No two people are exactly alike.

However, it can be safely said that the best way a funeral director can help his grief-stricken family is by his calm, unhurried, reassuring manner. They have confidence in his ability to serve them, hence his influence with them has greater effect than that of anyone else, unless it be the minister or priest. A funeral director's quiet manner can do much toward establishing calmness in the attitude of the bereaved. He should never talk more than necessary, should never attempt to dictate, but by tactful suggestion he can wield considerable influence and let them think the thought suggested was their own.

Often times a family has been comforted greatly by the funeral director saying, on the first call, "You can depend on us. If there is anything at all we can do for you before you come in to make arrangements for the service, just let us know."

In the discussion group referred to above, one funeral director said, "I have had just the same experience as was related a few minutes ago. I think if we are sympathetic and helpful that is all that is necessary. A funeral director can talk himself into more trouble than anything else he can do, and the less he says the better. Just a hand shake, probably a little extra squeeze of the hand—those little gestures mean more than anything he can say. I think the less he says the better."

Another funeral director suggested: "Could you not say 'I am ready to help you now'?"

Another suggestion was, "I usually shake the hand with a warm grasp with a few words, 'We appreciate your confidence and want to help you in every way. Are there any telephone calls we can make for you?' Statements like that mean much to them."

One thoughtful funeral director of wide experience had this to say: "One of the most important things about the first call, of course, is your first start, and then be a good listener. If the funeral director can sit and listen and let them unburden themselves to him, making a slight exclamation now and then, such as "I have never heard anything like that before," it is very important. If he listens, sits there and is patient, they are going to tell how efficient he was in taking care of things.

"The next thing, as you leave, linger just a minute after the body has been taken out of the house, and let them know that you are going to take every care of mother in every way that you know how. Just that last assurance, with the hold of the hand, will make them feel so differently when they see mother's body leaving."

It must be remembered, however, that no two families, in fact no two people, can be treated exactly alike. As one funeral director expressed himself: "You have to feel your way along and act as your experience with people guides you to act."

More and more deaths occur in hospitals and other such institutions, and in these instances we seldom see the family. They have usually left before we arrive for the body. In these instances it is often a good plan to contact them either by phone or personally calling at the home, offering to assist in any way possible, by helping prepare the newspaper obituary form or any other assistance they might need. Often they have left word with a nurse that they will call at the mortuary at a certain time, in which case nothing need be done toward contacting them until they arrive at the mortuary.

On leaving the home with the body, however, it is always well to let the family know that a car will call for them whenever they are ready to come to the mortuary to arrange for the service, if they wish. Often a family will say, "We do not know what to do, as this is our first experience." Many feel at a loss as to what to do who may not express themselves.

Family Comfort

Many mortuaries leave a little explanatory booklet with the family when the call is at the home, or take it to them at a convenient time when the call has been to a hospital. Such a booklet explains briefly the things the family must do and the information they must know in attending to the arrangements, completing the certificate, the obituary, etc.

When the family arrive at the mortuary, this may be their first visit to a place of this kind and they feel like "strangers in a foreign land." This feeling adds weight to their already helpless state. They must be put at ease by a kindly, helpful attitude on the part of the person greeting them as they enter.

The arrangement room, of course, should have comfortable chairs so that the members of the family can relax and rest physically during the time they are there. It should be restful in appearance and, above all, must be well lighted. There should never be any dark rooms or dark hallways for a family to see while they are in a mortuary building. The walls of the arrangement room as well as those of other rooms open to the public, should be finished in a quiet, soft color, preferably a pastel shade, and thus be as restful in appearance as possible.

Needless to say, every room in a mortuary must be clean and well kept. This fact is probably more true of the rest rooms. Many will judge every part of the establishment by the cleanliness of these rooms, which should be spotlessly clean, every inch of them.

Most family groups making the actual arrangements are small, just a few persons. The room should not be too large and the chairs should be quite close to the desk of the funeral director, for persons like to sit close when talking and planning the arrangements for the service. If they feel too far away they will pull their chairs closer. This is a natural psychological reaction, the same as would be felt in a doctor's office, in a clergyman's private study, or anywhere that things are discussed that are of a nature very intimate and close to their feelings. Chairs should be near the arrangement desk.

Funeral Director's Influence and Help

In the arrangement office is possibly the most convenient place for the funeral director to influence the family toward a calm attitude by his own manner of speech and action. He must never appear hurried. He must allow ample time in talking to them. He must allow them to decide every phase of the service. Suggestions, of course, are helpful, especially if asked for, but he must never attempt to tell a family what they should do. It is their matter to decide; he is to serve them according to their wishes.

In making arrangements for the service most families have a general idea of what they want. The funeral director is to see that nothing is omitted, of course, that should be a part of a service. Many times they want suggestions from him and need his guidance as to what should be done. He is their counselor. Here lies the opportunity for him to influence them to maintain the high standards throughout the arrangements of the services that should be maintained, that are in keeping with accustomed standards in their living.

There are many details that are part of every funeral service. Tabulations have been made as to the number, but probably the number is not exactly the same for any two services. Nevertheless, they are many, and the hours required to complete them occupy the attention and thought of the mortuary staff and the family throughout the time between death and final disposition.

While we can not forget any one of the many details to be arranged for a service, neither can we allow ourselves to become mechanized in making these arrangements with people who depend on us to help them express their sentiments, their emotions in this service. Let us repeat over and over, this is not "just another case" but a most tragic experience in the lives of the bereaved family.

Casket Selection

When the family are shown the caskets they must be allowed ample time to make their decisions. Usually, in their unsettled frame of mind they are not capable of hurrying. The funeral director should be able to explain the construction of every item of merchandise he has as well as the various types of material used in their construction. He should not, however, attempt to explain something he does not himself understnad, but it is his duty to know these things.

The period spent in the casket selection room is one of the most difficult for most persons. They are in a strange place and they are there to select merchandise with which they are not familiar and which they do not want to buy but are forced by circumstances beyond their control to buy. "Well-meaning" friends who come along to "help" usually prove to be the biggest problem a funeral director and the family have to face. Such friends, many times, have to be "sold" before the family can or will decide. These friends usually do not have the necessary sentiment or feeling in order to properly evaluate the wishes or the needs of the family. To too many of these "friends" it is merely a "practical" matter to be disposed of as simply and conveniently as possible. More care and tact is required with these people, often-times, than with the members of the family themselves. However, it is seldom that persons outside the family intrude on family privacy to this extent.

Whether or not a funeral director admits it, his prices are an integral part of his public relations program. There is not a funeral director anywhere, perhaps, who is not called upon to serve families on all financial levels. His service being the same regardless of merchandise pur-chased, he must be able, through this merchandise, to satisfy the needs and desires of all families, or as nearly so as is possible for him to do. His prices, therefore, must be so established that he can satisfy those from the lowest to the highest incomes of his community. It is good policy to see that everyone who enters and leaves the selection room knows his range of prices; let them know that, regardless of financial circumstances, every family he serves will be properly served with suitable merchandise and adequate service. This is a necessary part of every funeral director's public relations program.

While this treatise is not to enter into the merchandising or cost accounting phase of funeral service, let us here inject one thought because it affects a funeral director's mental attitude toward those he serves, and that attitude is important psychologically. Regardless of the so-called "average" overhead cost of a service, let it be considered merely a relative term. It is a mistake to talk in terms of "loss cases," "break-even cases," and "profit cases." When there are so many funeral services a year conducted by every funeral director, the gross income is the sum total of all sales and the net profit is the difference between the total of all costs and that gross income. Regardless of its price bracket, each funeral service contributes to that gross income. It is the sum total of all services, rather than the individual service in itself, that determines income. If a man allows his costs to reach unjustifiable levels and is a poor manager, then even the so-called "profit cases" will not earn him a profit. The idea is this, that regardless of the financial status of an individual family being served, the funeral director's mental attitude must be to give the best service possible.

In the final analysis, the average American family will buy within its means to pay and that is the important thing. The transition which has taken place in the funeral profession in these United States in the past century has approximately paralleled the social and economic trend. The preparation of the dead, attention to the bereaved, funeral merchandise, funeral housing, practices in funeral procedure have all been developed step by step, by experience, observation, imagination and creative effort, the same as service in other fields has been developed. The present technique of this profession is the result of seeking through trial and error to find and satisfy public desire. Present methods, facilities and merchandise exist because the public has found in them values it has been willing to pay for in spite of the necessary sacrifice of other things.

Are these values real? Do they spring from higher and finer motives? Do they lift and inspire? Are they worth what they cost? The answer is found in the reactions of the public. If the public accepts these things, prefers these things, the answer is in the affirmative. The public reaction while in the casket selection room probably gives the answer more clearly than it could be reflected anywhere else about the mortuary.

Probably the two most important things regarding the display are: (1) The price steps must be kept uniform, an easily ascended progression of prices, making it easy for buyers to move from one price to the next; (2) The funeral director must know facts about the materials and workmanship of the caskets and vaults he buys and sells. The public is becoming more material-conscious as a result of technological developments.

The selection of a casket is the most difficult of all arrangements that must be made for every funeral service for the grief-stricken family. The sight of the caskets immediately brings to their minds the thought that soon they will see the body of their loved one lying in one of these caskets. The use of more color in the construction and styling of present-day caskets has done much to minimize the drabness and somberness of these articles of merchandise. Color means life, and this uplifts the feelings of the bereaved. They may be entirely unaware of this influence, but it exists, nevertheless.

Many funeral directors leave the selection room at some time during the time the family is looking at caskets, and remain away for a few minutes. This allows members of the family better opportunity to talk over matters, financial or otherwise, which may be a help in making a decision. Since about 87% of our impressions are obtained through our sense of vision, perhaps such a plan is usually a wise one.

As long as people admire beautiful things we need not fear their desire for the beautiful in our service and merchandise. If our service meets their needs effectively, if our merchandise holds the desire for quality in eye appeal, we need have little fear for our future. People accept whatever they are educated to accept. It is the task of those in the funeral profession to educate the public in the right paths. The public will respond in the right way to the right kind of appeal in our service and our merchandise.

It is this desire for beauty, plus the fact that living flowers represent life, plus social pressure of doing the accepted thing, that leads to the desire of people to send flowers to the funeral services. Such acts serve as an emotional outlet, also, being an expression of affection toward the grief-stricken survivors and a tribute to the memory of the departed. The absence of flowers robs the funeral service of the beauty and impressiveness which so often tends to ease the burden of sorrow by their presence. Flowers truly belong to every setting that wants to be beautiful and impressive, and no one can deny that a funeral service has these elements, or should have.

The arrangement of the flowers is an art in itself. The only phase of that work that deals directly with psychology is the handling of these flowers and seeing that there is no clash of color in the arrangement. The people who paid their money for the flowers want to see them treated with care, placed carefully. The flowers represent the affection felt toward the memory of the departed and the surviving family; they are a memorial; they have personality. They must be handled with care, even reverence.

Public Relations Begin at Home

In concluding this discussion of our public relations, let us consider a few more factors which are vital and should receive serious consideration.

It has been said by some funeral directors that the people of a community hold their chosen mortician in high esteem but do not think so highly of funeral directors in general. This is no doubt true to some extent, but it is also true that a man cannot think highly of one funeral director without having his opinion raised of all funeral directors. The public relations program, therefore, for the entire profession begins right at the doorstep of each one of us. If I can hold the esteem and respect of my friends, of those in my own community, then my own portion of the program is fulfilled. But **I must begin at home**.

This is the best and only permanent good will building program we can practice. In this way we can present truths to the public that they can learn in no other way. In this way we will gain and hold public confidence and esteem for all morticians.

It is true that people will listen more readily to sensational lies than they will to truths. The sensational "debunker," the demagogue and rabble-rouser are more dramatic figures than the sober advocates of fact. Their misstatements can be accepted without thought, and most people have a congenital aversion to thinking. This places morticians in the position of presenting truths to overcome public ignorance. This is a position similar to that of a school teacher who knows and believes in his subject but who must find attractive ways to impress it indelibly upon his pupils. Our class consists of many millions of pupils, and the task of educating them is one that cannot be accomplished overnight. But the only way it can be accomplished is in each individual community.

The local mortician is usually a leading figure in community and social life through civic activities, church, fraternal and club organizations. He is never an isolationist. His fellow citizens know him, call him by his first name, work with him in organization work, see him as he answers the calls of need in the community regardless of the time of day or night, every day of the week, never refusing because of lack of finances on the part of a family or the cause of death. He is never "too busy" to serve a bereaved family.

No amount of publicity will change the opinion of the citizens of a community about their chosen funeral director. If he conducts himself as a true professional man, if his integrity is beyond reproach, if he is personally well-liked and respected, then the entire profession will be viewed favorably by the citizens of his community. If the contrary is true of this one funeral director, then the opposite view will be held by his citizens, and no amount of publicity can change it.

The funeral director, like all other professional and businessmen, is influencing public opinion every hour of every day. The way he treats his friends, his neighbors, his employees, his clients, will affect public opinion of him and, equally of the profession as a whole. Each one has the responsibility of winning the favorable opinion of his own community toward the entire profession as well as of himself. All must work together to insure that the truth about the profession becomes common knowledge.

A satisfied public is the only guarantee of a permanent future. And the only safe way to grow without additional overhead expense is to have the public boosting for us, people working for us who are not on the payroll.

Danger in Carelessness

A mortician's greatest danger is at that time when **he feels himself as being entirely successful,** because it is at this point that he will become careless, he will not watch quite as carefully the little details of service, those little things that means so much to the bereaved family. He will lose the "common touch." He will not feel the "humility" that is so necessary in all service attitudes. At this point he is a failure.

Favorable public opinion for the funeral service profession can be had only by every mortician seeing to it that his public is given favorable news about him, and that he gives no opportunity for any unfavorable publicity, either from the service he renders or from anything he does or says. Scandal or slander is sensational news and is so easily publicized that it is practically impossible to eradicate from public opinion the impressions gained from such news. It is from such beginnings that attacks are made on established funeral customs and upon the funeral profession as a whole. Unfortunately, the undesirable are most aggressive in seeking public attention and favor. The innumerable valuable services given every day by sincere morticians are forgotten in the face of an unfavorable item of comment. It is the responsibility of every funeral director to see that no damaging propaganda has a chance to emanate from anything he says or does.

Public opinion is based on the education of the public, which believes what it is told.

One further step can be taken. In addition to every mortician sincerely rendering proper service to his clients, he can and must cooperate with his fellow morticians. The entire group must present a united front, which can be done only through organized effort.

Human Relations Hazard

Probably the commonest human relations hazard is the seeming inability of the average person to **put himself in the other fellow's place**—to see situations from another's point of view. Nearly everyone will recognize this as a fact, but the tendency is always to apply it to the other person, not to oneself. In other words, the other person should "see my point of view." Often there is too little effort made to see the other person's point of view.

This failing is common to employer and employee, to buyer and seller, between competitors. Whenever trouble arises between two persons, the common habit seems to be to place the blame on the other person. Employer will blame employee, employee will blame employer, when in many instances there has just been a failure on the part of both to understand the other's viewpoint, failure to concede anything by either of the persons.

Personnel relations are now receiving much more

attention than ever before because it is realized there must be harmony throughout an institution or an industry in order to maintain efficiency, and efficiency benefits all concerned. The employee must be contented and happy, with opportunity for advancement. The employer must feel that he is receiving value in return for wages paid.

In past centuries the worker was born to a certain economic lot, his condition was drab, his opportunities did not improve. In America, however, there has been developed the opportunity for self-improvement through study, ambition and education. Recent inventions—the machine age, education, organization—all these things are responsible for the improved position of the employee and his is a happier lot than ever before. The employer frequently was once the employee; the employee has ambition to eventually become the employer, or at least to improve his lot: We are only beginning to make progress in the field of human engineering. As education and opportunities increase, more progress will be made.

Any business must depend to a large degree upon the good will and mutual cooperation of the people within the organization. This good will and cooperation is particularly important to a service organization, such as a mortuary.

Personnel Pointers

The United States Chamber of Commerce Personnel Department has made specific suggestions for building personnel good will.

"Advise members of the organization of company policies. Make clear to everyone the principles and objectives you have in mind."

"Establish responsibility and authority. In so doing, it is important to combine authority with responsibility. It is also important that each worker understands his relationship to others above or below. Equally important is the matter of informing responsible people of any changes being contemplated."

This organization has also given a 6-point plan of facts which should be provided for everyone in an organization. They are:

1. "The background and purposes of the company."

2. "The standards of conduct and services expected of the employee."

3. "The employment rights and opportunities of the employee."

4. "Relationship with superiors, subordinates, and fellow workers."

5. "Procedure for dealing with employer-employee problems."

6. "Advance notice of changes in policies."

Because any mortuary public relations program depends to a large extent on proper personnel relationship and loyalty, whether it be a large or small mortuary, these points are emphasized here. Every employee represents his firm every contact he makes.

Because personnel relationships are so important to any service institution and because they so greatly affect proper public relationships there are several points that should be mentioned at this time. These include consultation, grievances, wages and classification, job security, social responsibility, training.

High morale frequently hinges on discussing the performance and work done by a person and giving proper credit for efficiency. The same applies to constructive criticism and the clearing up of misunderstandings. Another important factor is the proper consideration of suggestions for improvement made by an employee.

Opportunity and procedure must be provided for expressing and discussing employee grievances. Such grievances should be promptly and satisfactorily settled.

To be happy and efficient on his job each employee should have the knowledge that he is performing work for which he is best fitted by natural ability and experience. His wage should be commensurate with his skill. As he develops in skill and experience he should be considered for higher classification which will give him greater compensation.

Knowledge of reasonable regularity and continuity of employment is essential to personal efficiency. Terminations should be carefully considered and, except for serious cause, should be preceded by adequate advance notice to permit seeking other employment.

Employee productivity is increased through knowledge of a reasonable protection against accidents, sickness, old age penury, and economic disaster. This can best be provided by insurance, pension, hospitalization, and sick benefit plans.

A clear description of the duties to be performed and instructions in the best method of performance should never be neglected.

Regardless of the size of a firm, whether it be small or large, if it has one or more employees, there should be definitely defined policies regarding these employees. The basic ideas outlined in the preceding paragraphs can be applied in any mortuary. Good will is important and pays big dividends, but it has to be earned by common sense steps that will promote a feeling of security and loyalty.

Causes of Discharge

In several thousand cases examined there were found to be two major causes of termination of employment. These were (1) Lack of skill or technical knowledge; (2) Lack of social understanding.

Incompetence was the largest single cause. In the scale it accounted for twenty-five per cent of the discharges. Slowness and physical unadaptability stood at about four percent each. Lack of social understanding accounted for two-thirds of the reasons. Listed under this heading were insubordination, general unreliability, absenteeism, laziness, trouble making, drinking, violation of rules, carelessness, misconduct, dishonesty. These failings are more serious than lack of skill; skill usually can be learned or acquired readily. Change of habit is not so simple.

Contrary to popular opinion, the slower worker is much more inaccurate than the more rapid worker. In scores of tests made, without exception throughout the groups, slow workers were found to be correct in less than forty per cent of the tests, while fast workers were correct in eighty per cent of the tests. A similar relationship has been found to be true with regard to students during their examinations. The same can be said in the learning and retention of material.

Accuracy can be developed with speed. If a speedy

worker is inaccurate it is probably because he also is a careless person. Close attention to work being done is the factor that determines the efficiency of the individual.

Personalization

Funeral service is greatly personalized. Bereaved families usually look to some one person to serve them, particularly in the smaller communities. It seems that usually a family will feel more secure when served by the same individual throughout their contact with the mortuary. It is a highly personalized service.

Six Public Relations Rules

Dale Carnegie, the most widely read author in human relationships, sets forth several simple rules for the improvement of friendly relations with other people. His advice can be summed up in six simple rules for the average funeral director in his dealings with the people of his community. These seem to adequately conclude these remarks in public relations. These six rules, briefly stated, are:

1. Be genuinely interested in other people.

2. Smile. A man without a smiling face should never open his shop.

3. Remember that a man's name is to him the sweetest and most important sound in the language. Remember it and use it.

4. Be a good listener. Encourage others to talk about themselves and don't forget that many persons call a doctor when all they want is an audience.

5. Talk in terms of the other man's interests.

6. Make others feel important and do it with sin-

cerity.

The whole value of public relations can be summed up in these six rules of relationship with other people. . . .

Reverberations

Returning from a funeral service recently, a lady who was a close friend of the family of the deceased said to me, "Mr. Martin, did you read the article in Reader's Digest this month, entitled 'Death on Parade'?"

I replied, "Yes, I did."

She said, "You know, I agree in many respects with that man's view, that we should return to the simplicity of our forefathers in funeral services and funeral customs. I believe that funerals, of all things, should be very simple. Sometimes there is too much elaborateness, too much fuss, too much expense put into funerals."

I asked her just what part of the funeral service or of our present day funeral customs she thought we should start to simplify.

She replied that she would not want to see the body returned to the home after the embalming was completed, or to be left in the home; nor would she want a home funeral, because it was so hard on everyone concerned to have all of that commotion in the home.

I said to her, "As I have been told of funeral services a hundred years ago, even fifty years ago, they lasted some two or three hours and were not considered a success unless everyone was weeping and some of the women had fainted and others were hysterical, that the minister preached a regular "hell-fire" sermon. Compared to today's funeral service that is about thirty minutes in length, sometimes less, with the minister preaching a message that has as its sole motive the comfort of the bereaved, with the family in a private room away from the staring and curiosity of the public, I would consider today's funeral service much simpler than the funeral services of our grandfather's days.

"As to the statement that embalming should be eliminated, which was made in this particular article you mentioned, we would not want to return to the day when disease was so easily spread due to lack of this disinfection, and when the burial had to be held as soon as the grave could be prepared in the warm months."

"I would not want to see embalming eliminated at all," she hastened to say, "nor would I want a two or three hour sermon."

"Then just where would you start to simplify today's funeral services?" I asked her. "We would not want to do away with the automobiles and go back to the horse-drawn hearse, or the spring wagon that used to be used to transport the homemade casket to the cemetery. We would not want to go back to the custom of calling in a cabinet maker to measure the body and make the casket for every death. Present day caskets are much more comforting in their beauty and in their simplicity, leaving a much more comforting memory picture."

"No," she said, "I would not want to go back to any of those things."

"Then," I said, "that leaves the expense of the funeral, which is the thing many of these writers magnify the most. If we used grandpa's spring wagon and a team of horses, if we hired a carpenter to make a plain casket each time, if we left the body in the home from time of death until burial, if neighbors came in and dressed the unembalmed body, then we could eliminate the cost of today's funerals, for the most part. But, since we do not want to go back a century on any of these things there is no way of eliminating the cost of today's funerals. And, speaking of costs, the cost of funerals has not gone up as much as the cost of most items in the cost of living in recent years."

"That's right," she answered, "funerals have not gone up as much as many other items. I know that from experience."

"Modern conveniences must be paid for," I reminded her. "I really do not know how we can go back in any one part of our service in any way that the public would really approve. And as long as we must have these conveniences and services there is no way of cutting down on the expense of furnishing them."

"I guess you are right about that, Mr. Martin. I don't know where we would start if we tried to go back. And, after all, most of today's funeral customs are simpler than were those of the past."

"Just one more thought," I said, as we stopped at her door. "Just remember that few, if any, of these men who write these articles on funeral reform are reformers. Seldom does one of them actually try to do anything about the things he advocates. These writers are writing these articles for one reason only, and that is the money they get paid for having them published. They have no interest in actually trying to change anything."

"I hadn't thought of that," she answered. "I guess you are right in that."

While it is very poor policy to ever argue with anyone, yet it is often an easy matter to point out some of these truths to our friends who bring up the subject themselves.

CHAPTER XI

PRACTICAL CONSIDERATIONS

Embalming

It is the ability to preserve the dead human body so that final disposition might be delayed that marked the beginning of a new vocation less than a century ago. These men who took charge of this procedure were known as undertakers, probably because they were undertaking something which few people cared to attempt. At first it was only a sideline, because there was little to do except to take the ice box into the home, place the body in it until almost time for the funeral service, then see that it was dressed and placed in the coffin that a cabinet maker had made to fit the contours of the body. Usually friends and neighbors "laid out" and dressed the body.

From this crude beginning the old-time undertaker gradually accumulated more equipment in order to better serve those who called him. This is the American way of life, the desire to give better service, and has always been the guiding motive within the funeral profession.

Arterial embalming for funeral purposes was first practiced in order to bring Civil War soldiers home for burial. Previous to this time attempts at preservation by arterial injection were by physicians and for anatomical purposes only. By the beginning of the present century arterial embalming was beginning to make considerable headway. Men were using the term "embalmer" and were offering their services to the public the same as other professional men were doing. As advancement was made in this new art its acceptance became more widespread and its progress more rapid.

Present day embalming permits funeral services to be delayed as long as necessary for distant relatives to attend, permits the body to be sent long distances for burial, all of which means much to the public. Today's embalmer has done more to prevent the spread of disease in his community than most people realize. However, the appearance of the body is the thing people see in his work and this is the thing that is the most appreciated. It is this that has stimulated the advancement and the acceptance of the funeral profession as a distinct service.

If the embalmer were not able to preserve bodies, to perform his service so that these bodies present the appearance of naturalness and health, erasing the effects of sickness and suffering, there would be little need for a funeral profession. This is the foundation, the most important part of the memory picture that is to comfort those who mourn. This affords the bereaved family the opportunity of arranging a funeral service that will be a thing of beauty and impressiveness. This makes possible the building of the entire funeral service structure. That this part of the service has met the desires and the needs of the public is proven by the structure that has been built upon it.

The whole public relations program, then, depends on the ability of the embalmer to give the public the one thing it wants more than anything else from the funeral profession, a lifelike appearing body. Given this, a family will spend much time in the reposing room in the presence of the body, and their appreciation will be great, indeed.

Aside from the comfort obtained from a lifelike appearing body, most people receive the most satisfaction from the religious part of the funeral service. A service that is in keeping with their religious beliefs means much to the grief-stricken survivors. Most religious beliefs give promise of a future life of happiness and of reunion, that earthly separation is only temporary. In their feeling of helplessness and dependence in their loss, such beliefs give them an untold amount of comfort and courage.

There can be no closer relation than exists between funeral services and religion. Funeral services **are** religious services. Every well-regulated funeral establishment works closely with the clergy, and clergymen in return welcome the opportunity to work closely with the funeral director.

It is part of the training of every funeral director to know and understand religious rites and ritual. It should also be part of his training to understand the symbolic significance of every part of the religious ritual connected with the funeral service. While the contacts of many funeral directors are predominantly, and sometimes almost exclusively, particularly in large cities, with certain groups and certain religious denominations, every one of them is called occasionally to supervise a funeral outside of his own special sphere. This is particularly true in small communities where one funeral director must serve all religious groups within his community.

Both the funeral director and the clergy are called because there is the need felt for the comforting services which they are expected to give. Both must work together, each performing his own duties and not encroaching upon the duties of the other.

Since there can be no complete, successful outlet for the strong emotion of grief, representing the completely helpless state that it does, then there must be some means of comfort to soothe the perturbed minds. The comfort of the religious service, provided by the faith of one's choice, is the best means of providing a substitute for an outlet for pent-up feelings within the grief-stricken individual. It is the symbolism of the religious service that comforts the troubled minds.

There must be a ceremony to consummate all relationships, whether it is being initiated into an organization, christening a baby, getting married, laying a cornerstone, or conducting a funeral service. The funeral service symbolizes the belief in a future life for the person upon the cessation of this earthly life; it is affirming the placing the welfare of the departed into the dominion of a higher power that will provide a better and a more abundant life than was provided on earth. This is a great comfort to most people and is the means of helping them maintain a normal mental equilibrium at a time when they are physically helpless to do anything. Since earthly relationships cannot be restored there is much comfort in the hope of the future as promised by present-day religious beliefs.

The purpose of the religious funeral service is primarily two-fold. First, it is a memorial, a tribute to the life and memory of the one now dead. Second, it is a promise of a just reward for the life lived, a justice that earthly life had not always provided, and it is a promise of future reunion of loved ones. This is, in a general way, the teaching of most present-day religions and it is a great comfort to those who accept them.

A definite ceremony or ritual, then, usually serves as a cushion to the shock of bereavement, to comfort and to encourage. Man is somewhat given to mysticism.

He will not be satisfied without some ritual. The funeral ritual is a formal, pubilc recognition and proclamation that the deceased has gone not to return. Though mystical in character it feeds reality.

The funeral service is for the living but it should honor the dead. Its merits are measured by the psychologic effects that the service leaves with the bereaved family and friends and the public generally. The idea is that the funeral service will be so directed that it will help to develop a feeling for the naturalness and dignity of life and death and bring the maximum of comfort to the bereaved.

Most people are accepting death as a natural event in the course of living, just as birth is the natural way to begin this life, just as growth is a part of it, so is death the natural way to end it. This attitude, being the result of today's advanced knowledge of things, helps people to control their reactions and remain in a calmer frame of mind. They feel the grief suffered in the loss, to be sure, but their outlook on life being of a sane viewpoint, they are able to maintian a calmer mien.

The religious funeral service being symbolical of all that people believe and hold sacred, having in it all of the religious convictions and hopes held by them, the smoothness of this service is of paramount importance. Everything must be done to calm those in grief. A few practical suggestions are here in order, for this part of a funeral director's duties is of the utmost importance in establishing desirable public relations.

The Memory Picture

For the funeral director, the funeral service is the culmination of all previous efforts in his service to every family. At this time he is in the spotlight more than at any other time. The public does not see him as he performs his many other services for every bereaved family following a death, but the public does see him now, his every move. He and his entire service are now "on exhibit." It is a critical exhibit.

Needless to say, the funeral cars should all be spotlessly clean, every man on the service neatly dressed in conformity with those he is serving and the community in which he lives. The timing must be perfect if the service is to run smoothly; nothing can be done too early or late, but at the proper time. There must be no last minute confusion.

Punctuality is an absolute necessity. The family car must be on time in calling for the family, for there is nothing more trying than for a family that is already in an upset state of mind being made more nervous by having to wait and worry for fear the family car will be late, or perhaps is already late.

When the service starts, it is the minister's until he is through. Occasionally, either a minister or a funeral director will trespass on the other's part of the service or will try to tell him how he should plan it. The funeral director should always remain in the background as much as possible throughout every funeral service, thus avoiding confusion, and distraction to himself. The public knows who is conducting the service and does not like to see him make himself too conspicuous by attracting any more attention than is necessary. The day is long past when the old-time "undertaker" would solemnly march to the front of the congregation, tall silk hat in hand and held over his chest, dolefully announce the procedure for those present to follow in retiring. A well planned service needs no ostentatious directing.

Everything has been provided in the way of physical settings by the modern funeral director to take away as much of the sting as possible from the experience of death in a family. Occasionally some custom will mar the whole setting, some little act that might be well meant. One example of this might well be mentioned, although there may be some disagreement on this point. Reference is made to the practice of many funeral directors of lowering the casket a few inches after it is placed on the cemetery device over the grave. Some persons may not react unfavorably to this, but many do. Families have been heard to comment favorably when this practice had been stopped. Many ministers have been heard to comment unfavorably on the practice of lowering the casket, even if it is but a few inches, in the presence of the family. One said, "If you could see the agonized expression on the faces of the members of the family as they watch that casket going down, even if it is only a few inches, you would never do it again." One minister added, "Or if you ever experienced it as a member of a family." While nothing may be said against the custom, if it is established, the cessation of it will bring many favorable comments.

The funeral director should remember this one point, "Keep as inconspicuous as possible throughout every funeral service." A well-planned service will run smoothly with little obvious directing. Just as an efficient executive of a large corporation or business concern does not try to attend to every detail because his properly trained assistants take care of these things, so a funeral director who plans his services properly and trains his assistants properly need not try to run around hurriedly to see that everything is being done. A good director does not concern himself with any but his own duties.

Every service a funeral director conducts creates in the minds of the family, and all who attend, a memory picture. An impression is created in their minds that will remain there the rest of their lives. It will be a memory they will like to recall or it will be one they wish they could forget. If this impression on their minds, this picture created for them, is comforting to recall, then the mortician has succeeded; if their memory of the service is not comforting, then it was a failure.

An Emotional Outlet

The funeral service, everything that is a part of it, serves an an emotional outlet, not entirely satisfactory of course, for it can not bring back the life that has departed. But it is the best and most satisfactory outlet possible to attain, as witnessed by the fact that down through the ages mankind has placed great stress on some form of funeral ceremony, and also by the fact that in modern times the public has accepted the services offered by the morticians. So, it does serve as the most satisfactory emotional outlet possible to provide for the strong emotion of grief. The physical outlet of weeping, the mental relief in seeing the body in the appearance of health, the purchase of the funeral and accessories, the arrangement of the service which is really the memorial to the memory of the life just ended, all of these things are the best means of relieving the tension that is being suffered. Every person, no matter how cold some individuals may appear, does have some feeling of sorrow when death comes to one of his group, and the service held in accordance with the social and religious practices brings a feeling of satisfaction.

Every part of the modern service is planned to

comfort the bereaved. The clergy of today have briefed their portion of the funeral service so that it is not the long, tiring ordeal it once was. They have changed the content of the message so that the primary motive is comfort rather than the harrowing emotionalism of the past. The music for a funeral service is becoming more comforting than past generations experienced. The effect is to quiet and soothe the feelings of the grief-stricken.

Music

Music is a live factor in our modern civilization and should play an important role in human life, especially in the time of great sorrow. Music has always been one of the greatest effecting agents on the emotions of man. The use of proper music during the funeral service not only adds to the value of the external features of the service, but also may be said to "tune in" with the subconscious mind to the extent that the conscious mind is assisted toward a release from its tension.

The fact that most persons seek music as a means of enjoyment, relaxation, and that this attitude seems to be quite universal among all people, proves that it is very influential in the lives of all persons. From the earliest times mankind has developed some sort of music. It fills psychological needs. It intensifies the sense of living. For most persons this means an emotional experience. In other words, music calls forth in man feelings of expectation and of satisfaction, and brings sensation of relaxation or of stimulation; it fulfills vital psychic and social needs.

While the selection of musical numbers for the funeral service itself should conform to the wishes of the family, usually the funeral director or organist is free to select the numbers to be played immediately before and after the service. This should be done with care.

In recent years many mortuaries have a continuous playing of subdued music recordings throughout the day. This is probably helpful to those visiting the mortuary, either to a service or a viewing. Psychologically it should have a soothing effect.

Higher Service Standards

There was a time when the funeral service was not a success until all present were in tears. The modern service sends them away quieted and comforted. How much more healthful this is for the physical bodily organism, when heightened emotions that have no satisfactory outlet build up tension within the body that can easily be too much to bear! Any service that can lessen this internal strife is of great value.

The funeral director is, throughout the making of all arrangements for the service, the family counsellor. This is his primary public relations opportunity and duty, to arrange for them a satisfactory service. They want to observe the customs that are prevalent in their communities and in their churches, and they depend on the funeral director to guide them, as well as to carry out their wishes. He can not dictate at any time, but he can make proper suggestions. It is his responsibility to assist every bereaved family he serves to properly plan a satisfactory service.

The only way in which the standards of the funeral profession can be raised, the only way in which the grief-stricken can receive the greatest degree of comfort, is through the avenue of the services of the mortician. Without the service the merchandise is of little value and there would be very little needed. It is service that has built the funeral profession to the high plane upon which it rests today and it is only through improved service, more intelligent service, that it will be possible to continue this upward trend.

It is only through improved service that a more satisfactory release of tension can be had, which serves a better emotional outlet. This is the mortician's most important public relations program, one upon which he will build a permanent structure, one that will stand for all time.

CHAPTER XII

THE NATURE OF FUNERAL SERVICE

Individual Response

It is not what happens that counts nearly so much as the way we respond to our environment. Our personal reaction to a situation is of much more importance than the situation itself. Our heredity we cannot help, and we can do little about our environment, but we are entirely responsible for our reactions to our experiences.

This principle applies to the progress of our funeral service profession just as surely as it applies to any individual person. Every funeral director and every emblamer is responsible for the future welfare of the profession. If he has within him the determination to improve his skills in his service to the public, to those who have confidence that he is serving them to the best of his ability, then the future is bright for the individual and the profession. On the other hand, if he is content to just "get by" (if there is any such thing as just getting by), to follow the course of least resistance by putting forth as little effort as possible in his service and in improving his skill, then the future is not bright, for the public will soon learn the facts and will lose confidence in him. The public can not long be misled or deceived.

The fact that the members of the funeral service profession have consistently improved their service in the past is quite good evidence that they will continue to do so, and will thus continue to merit public approval and support, and to maintain public confidence. The fact that the public has continued to accept improvements in service, even though these improvements meant additional cost, is proof that the public wants the best and will continue to demand the best. The competition of private enterprise is a reasonably good guarantee that the best will always be furnished.

Progressive trends in funeral service are the result of public desire as this desire is sensed by the mortician. If the public did not desire the type of service the mortician offers, such services would not be offered, or they would soon cease to exist. Funeral service in America, for example, is just as much a part of "The American Way of Life" as is any other principle that contributes to that prevailing mode of living. Our progress and advanced position in modern civilization is characterized by a great many facts, among which is the outstanding example that no people on earth pay such devotion to and respect for their dead as do we Americans.

Reverence for the dead has been an outstanding characteristic of people who have, in all ages, represented the highest degree of civilization. Anyone who doubts this statement can study history and he will find that it was those people, those nations who showed the deepest respect for their dead who also possessed the highest type of civilization, who made the greatest contributions to the world in every way. Care of and respect for the dead go hand in hand with all other advances. If America were to begin to slip in this respect it would be an indication of decadence in every part of living.

The fact that other nations have begun to adopt American funeral customs is the best indication that they are looking to America to set the pace for them. This is evidenced by the desire for embalming being on the increase among the more progressive peoples of the world, particularly the English speaking sections of the world, as well as in the increased use of casket coaches for funeral services and the increased directoral service by those who are becoming funeral directors as we know them in America. The increased desire for more helpful service to bereaved families is following the established custom practiced in the United States. American high standards meet human needs and desires more completely, otherwise they would not be copied. May America ever keep them high!

The modern funeral director has constructed his mortuary so as to eliminate the dull and gloomy as an appeal to the sense of beauty, and in expectation of breaking down the barriers of frustration and grief that come with the termination of intimate relationships. Good body appearance is paramount to the embalmer. Psychologically, it is necessary to overcome the mental attitude of the grief-stricken, which is associated with definitely unpleasant experience, through good body appearance, service, kindness, dignity and reverence. There is continually more emphasis being placed on the esthetic appeal.

Professionalism

There is one factor that is necessary for the consideration and decision of every member of the funeral profession. That is, are we really professional? The one element that marks a professional man above all other considerations is, does he personally serve those who call him for service?

Observing professional people—doctors, nurses, lawyers, dentists, pharmacists, clergymen, architects, and many others in specialized vocations—we note they have a common characteristic. When a client calls on any one of them to provide service they personally deliver that service. Also, most of them leave unprofessional activities and routine matters to their assistants.

Merchandising has its important place in every mortuary, naturally, but without the service there would be no funeral profession. It is for his service that the mortician is called upon by his patrons in their time of need. Merchandise, while a necessary item, is incidental to the service.

The individual operating a funeral home should be licensed and he should personally serve as many of his families as possible. If he cannot take care of all the professional activities, then licensed employees should be engaged to assist him. However, the mortician should imitate other professional people by serving his clients himself, insofar as it is possible for him to do.

There are other elements entering into the making of a profession. Probably the second most important element is that of educational standards. Many trades require more educational preparation than the funeral directing and embalming laws of many states require. We call ourselves professional, but are we, when in a short period of time, with none of the so-called higher learning required in some states, anyone can become a licensed funeral director and a licensed embalmer? Until academic college training is required we have no profession as professions are recognized by public standards. The states that have adopted years of college plus the period of practical training are entering into professional status for their funeral directors and their embalmers.

Another element of professionalism is the basis for charges. When patrons are sold a casket with nothing being said of service, the funeral director is a merchant, a businessman, not professional in any respect. If service charges as such are not sufficient to pay for the service given, if the casket is made to carry the load, the mortician is not professional. Regardless of the system of pricing a standard funeral service to patrons, they must understand that the one thing they are receiving above all else is service; they must understand that the one thing for which they are being charged in its proportional share is the service they are receiving. If this is done, then the mortician is a professional man.

In thinking of professionalism, let us consider briefly some general characteristics.

A person to be professional must have as his dominent motive that of rendering human service. He must have a deep sense of social responsibility. He must feel that the occupation which he enters is the thing he would rather do than anything else, both because it is the service which he would like most to render and because it is the thing he is most capable of doing. It is his "calling." The word "profession" meant originally "bound by a vow, a public avowal, to follow a calling." Hence the word "professor."

It is possible for a person who is not truly professional to become a member of a profession. Each profession should screen out those within its ranks who do not measure up to the necessary sense of social responsibility. Each profession sets its own standards and determines the qualifications to which aspirants must qualify.

A professional man must have, not only the desire, but the ability and the thorough preparation necessary to render human service. This means he must have physical energy, emotional stability, high intellectual skill and honesty, and the desire and ability to search for truth and to use it when found. A member of a profession is a specialist in some phase of service to society.

A professional man must join with those of his profession in the sharing of problems, findings and experiences; in organized cooperation for the better performance of service to society; and for the common welfare of the members of the profession. To this end members of a profession join in conferences, clinics, and conventions and in the publication of studies, papers, bulletins and journals. In other words, a profession is a group enterprise. It is democracy at work in a given occupation.

In summary, the three main characteristics necessary in a truly professional person are:

(1). A predominating sense of human service;

(2). Intellectual ability to put in thorough and prolonged education and training for the job;

(3). Consciousness of the fact that a profession is a group enterprise and as such demands of its members cooperation in the sharing of problems, findings, and experience and in promoting the welfare of its members.

The question might here be asked: What has this to do with the psychology of funeral service? The families who need the services of a mortician need the personal services of a highly trained specialist who will be able to serve them properly and intelligently, who can create for them the comforting memory picture that they expect and need. The psychological element is the proper mental attitude of the mortician in giving this service.

The family a mortician is serving should be made to feel that he is assisting them to show proper and socially-acceptable respect to the departed. The important thing is how well his services can be used to make the family believe they are giving unlimited expression to their own sentiment.

While it may seem trite in statement, so simply is it stated, the fundamental rules for successfully serving can be summed up as follows:

1. Learning what people like;
2. Doing more of it.
3. Learning what people do not like;
4. Doing less of it.

Determining the Future

What we do today determines what tomorrow will bring. If funeral directors and embalmers continue to serve the public to the best of their ability, the public reaction will be that of continued confidence and there need be little fear of outside encroachments. If an attitude of carelessness and indifference should creep into our service, the public will be quick to sense it and will quickly turn to any other service agency that appears to offer them the things they want and need. The future of the funeral profession is every day determined entirely by the desire and the ability of the funeral director and embalmer to give to those they are called to serve the type and quality of service they have every right to expect.

The proper mental attitude of everyone affiliated with the funeral profession toward the bereaved family will prompt him to watch for "little things" he can do to help them, little acts of kindness, little courtesies that they might not ordinarily expect. It is these so-called little things that are really the most important. The act of going to a little extra trouble to make a body look a little nicer, to make a member of a family a little more comfortable or more at ease, taking a little extra time and patience when he is in a hurry, these are, in general, the "little things" that are the most appreciated by those in grief and by the public.

Comparing successful and unsuccessful men of all vocations it is usually apparent to the observer as to why one is successful while the other is not. Their qualities are probably so intangible that it is difficult to find a sharp boundary line between the two, but the one will satisfy his clients to a greater degree than the other. Some decisive differences do appear. The successful ones make it clear that they are interested in their clients, they like people, they are honest, they are willing to go out of their way to accommodate and to treat all alike. The less successful are inferior in these points. The way the public feels toward them reflects the way they feel toward people.

In practical dealings with people, suggestion is the best form of assistance. Suggestion is an indirect procedure whereby one person affects the thought, feeling or behavior of another, while the other person feels all the while as if he were deciding for himself. It is giving advice without insisting on its adoption. One person directly telling another what to do appears to be placing himself above the other person, as intimating that the other person is not competent to guide himself. It violates his want for recognition. The funeral director is the family counsellor; it is his duty to help them to the extent that they need help, not to tell them what to do. He should suggest if needed, never dictate.

Ethics

There is another important consideration that should

receive attention here because it reflects mental attitude quite intimately, and that is the principle known as **ethics**. Ethics is defined here as "the rules of conduct recognized in respect to a particular class of human actions." Technically, ethics is a system of morality. Practically, ethics is the mental attitude of the individuals engaged in a common pursuit, toward one another and toward those they serve. Fundamentally, ethics is human conduct.

Professionally, ethical standards accepted by those engaged in a particular profession mean that any action on the part of one member of the profession works toward the general welfare of all persons so engaged as well as for the general public welfare. What is good for one individual to do must also be good for every member of the profession to do.

The commonly accepted ideal for all to follow is commonly known as The Golden Rule, "To do to others as you would have them do to you." While this is acknowledged by all persons as the ideal course of action, its interpretation is too often forgotten by too many persons under the stress of temptation, in individual instances, where temporary gain may be had. All persons declare this as the ideal course of action, but too often it is not followed. The fact that it is recognized universally is demonstrated by the fact that this principle is contained in every one of the world's religions. All people the world over, down through the ages, have realized this principle as the ideal course for all to follow.

One observer said, "It appears that much of the wrong-doing in the business world, as elsewhere, is done not because the doer means to do wrong, but because he believes it is 'all right' **for him**." A member of one of our state licensing and examining boards said, "Don't ask for anything for yourself that you would not want your competitor to have." This is quite an accurate rule to apply to every one of us.

As long as funeral service ethics are interpreted individually there will be firms and individuals who will do what they think is ethical according to their own interpretations. Ethics can not be interpreted individually; it must be interpreted as applying to every member of the profession. If a course of action is not good for every member to follow, then it is not good for one individual to follow. Just as a drop of ink in a pail of water makes the whole of the water cloudy, so an unethical act on the part of one mortician clouds the whole of public opinion about every mortician and the whole profession. The members of a profession determine the ethics of that profession by their own individual actions.

The question may now be asked, "What are the ethical and unethical actions recognized by the funeral profession?" "Is there a Code of Ethics for members of this profession?" There is a Code of Ethics as adopted by the National Funeral Directors' Association of the United States which, since its membership includes most of the funeral directors of the nation representing more than 85 per cent of the total funeral services annually, is in the best position to speak for the funeral profession as a whole. This Code should be carefully studied by all students and members of this profession and its principles very carefully adhered to.

CODE OF ETHICS

I

As funeral directors, we herewith fully acknowledge

our individual and collective obligations to the public, especially to those we serve, and our mutual responsibilities for the proper welfare of the funeral service profession.

II

To the public we pledge: vigilant support of public health laws, proper legal regulations for the members of our profession; devotion to high moral and service standards; conduct befitting good citizens; honesty in all offerings of service and merchandise, and in all business transactions.

III

To those we serve we pledge: confidential business and professional relationships; cooperation with the customs of all religions and creeds; observance of all respect due to deceased; high standards of competence and dignity in the conduct of all services; truthful representation of all services and merchandise.

IV

To our profession we pledge: support of high educational standards and proper licensing laws; encouragement of scientific research; adherence to sound business practices; adoption of improved techniques; observance of all rules of fair competition; maintenance of favorable personal relations.

* * *

As an affiliate of our state and national association, we subscribe to the principles set forth in the Code of Ethics and pledge our best efforts to make them effective.

(Signed) _ .

Every profession has its recognized Code of Ethics which every member is pledged to follow. By so doing, every individual member of that profession, the profession as a whole, and the public served, are all much better for such adherence. Let us again repeat, "A course of action that is good for all to follow is the best course of action for every individual to follow." There can rightfully be no exceptions.

In quoting the Code of Ethics of the National Funeral Directors' Association there is no intent to minimize those codes adopted by other organizations within the profession, each of which has its Code, similar in intent to that of NFDA. These other organizations, membership being by invitation, are banding together of funeral directors for the purpose of better service to the public through closer cooperation among themselves by the establishment of definite standards of practice within their own group, some by methods of research, all members of which subscribe to the Code of Ethics. These organizations all stand for improvement in service of the individual funeral director and thus of the profession as a whole, and are to be highly commended. Organized effort with high ideals always results in better standards and improved relationships among the members and with the public.

Associations

Every professional man should be an actively interested member of his local, state and national associations, adhering to the principles set forth by those organizations. It is only by cooperative effort, properly organized, that the most benefit can be gained, for the common good, both of the public served and the individual members of the profession. "What is good for all is also good for each individual." The sad fact is that there are always para-sites, there are always those who want a "free ride" with someone else paying the fare. One man says, "I don't need the association. I can get along fine without it," then proceeds to recount its faults and shortcomings. Probably he can, but it is only because there are others with sufficient wisdom, with sufficient concern for the general welfare, to devote the necessary time and effort toward the perpetuation of the organization. Without organized effort there would be no profession in existence today.

Association activity is the cooperation of the mem-bers toward the same common end, namely, that of better service to the public with more benefit to them-selves. It is an honest endeavor to arrive at a better understanding among themselves of their problems.

Whenever people understand each other there is little likelihood of trouble. If competitors would talk matters over more often, there would be little friction between or among them. They are all in the business of serving the public to the best of their ability, are intent upon making an honest living by continuing in business. Then, why not work as friends? As one man expressed himslef: "Life is too short for me not to be friendly with everyone, in-cluding my competitor." After all, what is accomplished by an unfriendly attitude? Nothing but furthering bad public relations, ill health, ill temper, all of which are bound to result in impaired service to the public.

One mortician made this statement, "Yes, that sounds nice; but remember that it takes two (or all) to cooperate on an agreement. My competitor just won't cooperate." It must also be remembered that "It takes two to make a fight or an argument." Men can cooperate and work together when they wish to do so. Frequent friendly visits help.

More business and professional men are working together and cooperating now than perhaps ever before because they have learned that such action is the best course,—that much energy and effort are wasted by working at cross purposes. There is also another reason for better cooperation, and that is the threatened invasion to individual private enterprise by socialism,—various socialistic plans in various and sundry forms. It is psychologically true that **it takes a common enemy to bring people together**. Members of a family may quarrel among themselves, but let an outsider intrude and they will unite against him. Will it take an invasion from another planet to bring the people of the world together?

Organizational efforts have continually become stronger in our country because the members who composed them have learned by experience that much can be accomplished for mutual good and gain by presenting the united front. Cooperation produces results.

The public will respect the individual mortician to the same extent that he deserves that respect and to the same extent that he respects his fellow morticians. It is through cooperative effort and understanding that the best and most consistent service can be given by a profession to the public it serves. All of this is not only fact, it is good psychology, for it interprets the proper mental attitude of the individual mortician toward everything pertaining to his service. These facts demand considerable study by every student and by every member of the profession.

CHAPTER XIII

PSYCHOLOGY IN ACTION

What Is Most Important

Much has been said about the most important aspects of our service. It might well be asked just what is the most important part of our service. This can be easily answered. The most important part of my service to a griefstricken family is **the thing I am doing for them at this very moment**. When I am on the first call, then at that moment this is the most important part of my service. When I get the body in my preparation room, then this is the most important part of my service. When I have the family in my casket selection room, the most important part of my service to them lies here. During the funeral service the most important part of my service to this family is the way I am conducting this service.

There can be no **most** important part of any funeral service, for to every bereaved family there is nothing that can be neglected. As long as the individual members of the funeral service profession follow this attitude consistently there can not be a great deal of criticism by those families served leveled against any mortician.

There is another element in the funeral director's service, however. It is one which is inherent within him, it is a part of him. It is his personality. This personality factor is the inherent quality upon which others base their opinions of a person. An individual inherits certain personality characteristics, then he develops these traits for better or worse. He can build them up or tear them down. It is these personality characteristics that will, more than any other one thing cause a man to be a success or a failure. Let it be said here that a man might fail in one vocation but succeed in another, due to his personality traits, his attitudes and aptitudes. His personality must be fitted to a particular type of endeavor if he is to succeed in it.

A person's attitude toward his work and toward people will determine whether he is a success or a failure in his particular calling. This attitude will build up or it will tear down his personality and his chances for making good.

As is pointed out elsewhere in this book, it is not what happens to us that counts but it is the way in which we respond to what happens. Individuals are not unhappy and depressed, or happy and gay, because of the people and things outside themselves. What is wealth to one is poverty to another; defeat to one, challenge to another. What does make the difference is our **inside** reaction to the **outside condition**. Self-pity, jealousy, anxiety, fears, excessive love of possessions—all states of unhappiness— are but the evidence of conflict and an admonition that something **within** us is out of gear. That something within must be overhauled. Human nature resists correction of self. It is much easier to shift the responsibility to some person or set of circumstances.

Freedom—the privilege of going wrong if we care to—is a great tax on our stability. It requires the ability to make wise choices and judicious decisions; freedom demands the setting up of standards and the willingness to assume the responsibility for carrying them out; it necessitates control of self, direction of self, and discipline of self.

It is our reaction to these circumstances, our attitude

toward our surroundings, that determines and sets our personality. An individual will inherit certain tendencies, but he can modify and change these tendencies if he so wills; in other words, he can mould his own personality in any way he wishes if he will only take the time and determination to do it. Every man is his own master in making of himself what he will.

What does this have to do with funeral service? Every funeral service establishment is managed by some individual or individuals. Each individual has a personality. To the public, to every family entering that establishment, the establishment is the individual person behind it. The mortician makes the mortuary what it is, it reflects his personality. Ours is a highly personalized service. A funeral home is the shadow of the funeral director in charge of it. That is why personality is so important to every one of us. That is why the greatest problem of public education is the mortician himself. It is he, each and every one in every city and community of our land, who is educating the public by his actions, by his attitudes, by his service, by his personality.

Public opinion of the funeral service profession is moulded by morticians themselves. Morticians make their own publicity, they determine their own destiny. They do this every day by their words and actions. All evil and all good about them come from within their own ranks, always.

Our greatest problem of public education is not the public; it is the funeral director who, through one overt or thoughtless act, tears down all the good public opinion which can be generated in months and years of conscientious effort. The public believes what it sees and hears from us and about us. Let no one of us ever give cause for unfavorable public opinion about funeral directors!

Personality

Since the stand has here been taken that personality is the strongest factor in the success or failure of the operation of a mortuary, let us analyze this item; let us see what it is and how it can be made to work for the betterment of the individual mortician.

Instincts and **habits** are the neural foundations of human activity. These are the bases of motivation. Instincts are inherited; habits are acquired. The two primary instincts are self-preservation and the perpetuation of the race. All of life's activities and habits can be formulated around these. Habits are, of course, learned reactions to stimuli. Without the efficiency of habits there would be no progress of any kind.

The behavior of every person depends upon four types of factors: (1) the inherited mechanisms, including quality of nervous tissue, sense organs, etc., (2) the acquired experience, involving the sum of habit patterns, (3) the physiological state of the body, and (4) the stimuli affecting his sense organs at the moment.

In studying personality and its development the observance of small children teaches much. Children are not inhibited by years of experience, have not acquired superficial attitudes, but are their natural selves more than are adults. They really correspond more closely to griefstricken families with whom the mortician must deal because at such difficult times these people show more of their basic personality than at perhaps any other time or in any other experience. Their grief has taken away acquired superficialities and the mortician sees them as they really are. Inherent desires are exaggerated, such as the desire of some to receive an unusual amount of attention, but in these actions are shown the personality traits of each individual as they are brought forth by strong emotional feeling.

In studying children it is not hard to see that one child is self-confident, another less so; one very active, another less active; one apprehensive and thinking always of himself, another ready to mix with others, do things with them, help and play cooperatively. Since a child's personality, his attitudes and modes of reaction, are all quite well fixed by the fifth year and do not undergo much fundamental change after that time, the importance of early training can be understood. An individual can, of course, correct flaws in his attitudes and reactions, in the faulty construction of his personality, if he understands them and exerts the determined effort for a sufficient period of time. This is not done in many instances, however, to any great degree, but early and inherent tendencies are not only allowed to continue but are allowed to grow and become more pronounced as the individual grows older. It is the usual thing that an individual's characteristics, his faults and his virtues, become more manifest with each year of age attained.

Adults are the result of their upbringing from infancy up through the years to maturity,—to chronological maturity, for many individuals never reach any other maturity than that of their years. A neurotic was not born a neurotic; he acquired this condition. The seeds were sown and cultivated in his home by those who disciplined him, or were supposed to discipline him. The bully was not born a bully, he acquired this attitude because of an intense inferiority complex, and his acquired method of overcoming this underrated feeling, of not wanting others to notice it, in that of forcing a superior feeling on others. Any man who is not kind to his subordinates is a bully and is trying to cover up an inferior feeling within himself. Any man who is a poor sport in a game is both a poor loser and a poor winner; no one can be one without also being the other. And it is largely the result of erroneous upbringing from childhood.

The neurotic attaches himself to someone who shoulders his duties for him; he insists upon the cooperation of others, but at the same time contributes practically nothing himself. Such a situation can arise only if an individual feels himself threatened by a defeat; when he has to a greater or lesser degree the vague impression that he is too weak, that he has no real value. Possibly he was raised a pampered child, with no effort required (other than perhaps a "tantrum") to obtain whatever he wanted, have it given to him. Nothing has value except as it pertains directly to his own whims and wishes.

Funeral directors are becoming more fully aware of the importance of psychology. Much of their success can be traced to the ability to deal with emotional upsets. Of related interest is an army report that 80% of men who "cracked up" emotionally never saw actual combat. The same thing, in principle, occurs at funerals. Some people just cannot stand up under emotional strain.

Improving Conversational Ability

One of the most important good will builders is the art of conversation. Conversational skill is an art that has a scientific and precise foundation. We will here present a few suggestions toward becoming a more interesting conversationalist.

First, train yourself to become a social detective. Look for good things in your companions, then pay a sincere and deserved compliment. People are starving for appreciation, but the average person doesn't pay one compliment a day to another person.

Second, learn to be skillful in what has been termed the "reversible why." Be deft. When someone asks a question you cannot or do not wish to answer, tactfully reverse the question. Above all, however, do not be blunt. If you are asked a question which requires a stand on a matter on which you do not wish to be committed, you can tactfully turn your answer so that the questioner will have to express his opinion.

A skillful conversationalist is one who can get other people to do most of the talking, and on subjects in which they are interested. By tactully probing around from one topic to another the other person can usually be induced to talk. A parent always likes to talk about his children or grandchildren. Most men like to talk about their business or some related subject. The subjects of entertainment, athletics, art, opera, literature, politics, are some in which most people are interested.

The most popular conversationalist, is, strange as it may seem, not the person who can converse on any and all subjects, or who knows all the answers. The most popular conversationalist is the person who is a good listener, believe it or not! All people like to be heard, they like to have their opinions respected, they like to tell their troubles, their experiences, they like to unburden themselves. They like the company of a listener.

More important than just listening is showing an interest in what the other person is saying. All people crave recognition, so a friendly interest in them can be assumed, even if it is not 100 per cent present. Show interest, look the person in the eye, even lean forward toward him; learn to converse modestly and quietly.

The other person will be pleased with the visit, will leave feeling more important and quite satisfied with himself.

The one paramount rule for friendly relationships with others is: Whenever you leave a person feeling more satisfied with himself as a result of his contact with you, he will like you. Introverts are not as popular as extroverts because they don't pay heed to the ego demands of their associates.

Ask another for information, advice or direction. Such a question is a sublte form of compliment. Psychologically, the questioner indirectly acknowledges the superiority of the questioned by coming to him for assistance.

Impute knowledge and experience to your associates whether or not you know they possess it. Such a compliment inflates their ego.

The tactful winning of young people consists principally in complimenting them upon the traits in which they aspire to excel. For middle-aged people, credit them with being healthy and spry. They wish to show that time has not affected them. For elderly people, credit them with looking younger than their years, or younger than others their age. Give them credit with retaining their ability in managing their affairs.

Social intelligence can be consciously cultivated. It depends on the possession of mental alertness or abstract intelligence. In developing it the items of recreational habits, etiquette, and complimenting others should be developed.

It all simmers down to this: **To make friends, be friendly yourself!**

Personal Traits

Let us now consider a few miscellaneous facts about our individual actions, little things that are normally overlooked in our everyday behavior, but things that are very important in our contacts with other people.

A psychologist has listed the common annoyances in people. It is worth noticing that 57 per cent of them all are things we do with our hands and feet, our manner of speaking and walking; 12 per cent of them relate to our clothing and to the way we wear it; 10 per cent are other physical characteristics that we can change if we will. Only 5 per cent include unchangeable features such as the size of a nose or the shape of the face or body. That adds up to 79 per cent (about 4 out of every 5 of our annoying characteristics) that have been learned and that can, therefore be eliminated by whatever means we use to break up bad habits.

We are all familiar with many of these little common annoyances, such as constant and frequent interruption by one indiviual of another when speaking, clicking of false teeth while talking, tapping of fingers or a foot, frequent clearing of throat, facial contortions, twitching of face or head, a hacking cough by persons who attend social functions, toying with nose or ear or hair with fingers, and innumerable other mannerisms, all of which are nervous habits that can easily be broken if the persons will to do so. Often times the individual who is guilty of such things does not realize he is doing them and least of all does he realize the annoyance they cause to others.

There is another type of common annoyance that hinders success in a business or a profession. It is that of the person who lacks feeling for relations among people. He is short on social wisdom. He is tactless, an egoist who behaves as if everybody but himself were insignificant. Such persons may be ever so capable, ever so intellectual, but they can never succeed because they irritate and antagonize everyone with whom they come in contact.

In contrast to the person who "knows it all" is the person who acts unsure of himself, and this, in the extreme, is probably worse. People do not care to be served by someone who lacks confidence in himself, who seems constantly uneasy.

The deepest principle in human nature is the craving to be appreciated. It is the most intense kind of wanting. The best-liked people are those whose whole manner and style of remark are a sort of flattery to those they meet, not to be over-emphasized but the sincere mannerism. If a man's manner and style of address are such that those he meets go away better pleased with themselves than when they came, he is the popular man.

Another characteristic to be developed is that of tolerance with all persons we meet and serve, tolerance with their faults and shortcomings as we might see them. We ourselves are not perfect, yet we desire that others overlook our own faults and praise us for our good qualities. We should do the same for others.

The best rule to follow in personal contacts with other people is to be always sincere and natural in cultivating traits that are acceptable and pleasing at all times. The best places to cultivate these traits are at home and in the office, with those with whom we come in constant daily contact. An individual's true personality is shown by his actions when alone in the presence of his family or co-workers. An even temperament, calm and unruffled under all conditions, is one to be cultivated.

It is not what happens that counts nearly so much

as the way we respond.

A Positive Attitude

A basic principle for success and happiness is a **positive attitude** by an individual. A positive attitude attracts, while a negative attitude repels. A great advance of Christianity over the old Jewish law was this element. Most of the Ten Commandments were negative; they said, "Thou shal not . . ." When Jesus taught he gave two commandments, and they were both positive: "Thou shalt . . . ." Perhaps that is one reason we have so much law breaking; the laws of our communities all say "Don't do this" and "Don't do that." A negative command calls attention to the thing that is to be avoided. A positive command calls attention to the thing that is desired to be done. A child that is told not to do so many things he wants to do is much more likely to get into trouble than the child that is told to "Come here and do this." He is going to think of the thing mentioned.

Isn't this attitude too often taken by morticians? How many pay more attention to the business their competitors are doing than they do to their own business? If more funeral directors spent all their energy on taking care of their own work instead of wasting so much of it on denouncing their competitors, if they paid strict attention to their own affairs and less to their competitors', all would be the better for it.

Evaluating one's business status in relation to a competitor's activity is not only bad, it is foolish. No one can mind his own business while attending to another's. Furthermore, by concentrating on what a competitor is doing a man makes his competitor his master. And no man can serve two masters.

This practice also is bad because it arouses envy. The funeral director who grabs the paper and turns to the death notices is not eager to find out who among the citizenry has died. He is only trying to discover how many calls his competitor has had. He is motivated not by curiosity but by envy. Every funeral director who envies a competitor begins to regard him not as a colleague who has an equal right to make a living, but as an opponent. And that attitude starts trouble.

Association effort, with the realization of the necessity of working together for survival and advancement, has made friendships among morticians, has caused them to realize that they are all working for a common goal and that much more can be accomplished by cooperation than by working at odds among themselves. **Cooperation brings success.**

Funeral Service Oath

I do solemnly swear, by that which I hold most sacred:

That I shall be loyal to the Funeral Service Profession, and just and generous to its members;

That I shall lead my life and practice my art in uprightness and honor;

That into whatsoever house I shall enter, it shall be for the benefit and comfort of those bereaved;

That I shall abstain from every voluntary act of misconduct and corruption;

That I shall obey the Civil Laws;

That I shall not divulge professional confidences;

And that I shall be faithful to those who have placed their trust in me.

While I continue to keep this oath unviolated, may it be granted to me to enjoy honor, in my life and in my profession, and may I be respected by all men for all time.

A

Abandonment, 164.

Academic, ii, iv.

Adler, (1870-1937; Austrian psychiatrist), 30.

Affection, 69.

"After Life," 167.

Agamas, (sacred scriptures of Jainism), 151.

Ahura Mazda, (deity of Zoroastrianism), 150.

Alcmaeon, (Greek philosopher and psychologist about 500 B. C.), 21.

Alexander the Great (356-323 B. C., King of Macedonia, conqueror of Greece), 22.

Allport (modern psychologist), 7.

American contribution, 29.

Anaxagoras (Greek philosopher and psychologist, 460 B. C.), 22.

Anger, 13, 69, 70, 71, 76, 78, 79, 89, 110, 114.

Animistic, Animism, (belief that inanimate objects have life or spirit), 16, 18, 143, 159.

Anxiety, 79.

Aristotle (Greek philosopher, 384-322 B. C.), 6, 7, 22, 64, 141.

Associations, 246.

Attention, 54, 59, 61.

Attitude, i, vi, 259.

B

Bacon (English philosopher, 1561-1626), 24.

Behaviorist (Stresses overt behavior), 30, 31, 66.

Beliefs, see Religion.

Bell (1774-1842; discovered reciprocal innervation and described the muscle sense), 27.

Bible, (sacred scriptures of Christians), 152.

Blushing, 28, 73.

Brahma (Hindu deity), 149.

Brain (the large mass of nerve tissue enclosed in the skull), 4, 5, 34, 47.

Bridge (genetic theory of emotion), 69.

Brown (1735-1842; introduced "suggestion"), 26.

Buddah, Gautama (founder of Buddhism, 560 B. C.), 151.

Buddhism, 140, 141, 151.

Burial, 166.

C

Cannibalism, 165.

Cannon, W. B., 77.

Christianity, 140, 141, 151.

Church, ii, 172.

Cicero (Roman orator, 116-43 B. C.), 23.

Classics (sacred scriptures of Confucianism), 152.

Clergy, 14, 172.

Columbus (discovered America, 1492), 24.

Compensation, 99, 100, 103.

Comte (1798-1857; introduced the term "sociology"), 26.

Concentration, 54, 55, 59.

Confucianism, 140, 141, 151.

Confucius, (founder of Confucianism, 551 B. C.), 151.

Confusion, 69, 89.

Bibliography

Psychology college notes from many sources.

Man the unknown, by Alexis Carrell

Anthropology, by Wallis

A Short History of Psychology, by Hulin

Managing Your Mind, by Kraines & Thetford

Psychology, by Shaffer, Gilmer & Schoen

The World's Living Religions, by Hume

The Small Sects in America, by Clark

The Great Religions, by Lyon

Manual of Funeral Procedure, by Myers

The Wisdom of the Living Religions, by Gaer

You and Your Grief, by Jackson

Notes from many addresses and discussion groups